KEVIN WICZER

Whispers from the Infinite:

CHANNELED MESSAGES FROM THE ETERNAL SOURCE

Published in the United States by GetKevInsight Press.

www.GetKevInsight.com

First Edition

ISBN (Paperback): 979-8-9936551-1-6

ISBN (eBook): 979-8-9936551-2-3

Thank you to Armando, Mom and Dad, my family, my friends, my spirit guides, my higher self, and all of those who have been a part of my continuing journey. Sending you so much love!

ABOUT THE AUTHOR

In May of 2024, I began a personal soul search. I felt lost and unsure of why. At the time, I was a playwright and theatre director, and I believed my life would always go in that direction. But theatre was slowly becoming more of an inner battle than a calling, and I didn't understand what was changing within me.

Someone introduced me to life path numbers, and from there I began listening to spiritual podcasts and reading metaphysical books. What started as simple curiosity quickly opened into a deep awakening. I chose to fully open myself to helping and healing others in any way my spirit guides wished to guide me.

A few months later, I received my first deck of tarot cards and began reading for myself, then for family, friends, and eventually others around the world. From these daily tarot pulls came the lessons that became my first book, *Divine Lessons from Your Guides*, written in collaboration with my spirit team.

In the middle of creating that book, however, I underwent a serious back surgery that required a three-month recovery. During that time, my want to pull daily tarot cards for lessons came to a halt. But something unexpected occurred.

While resting one morning, a video about automatic writing mysteriously appeared in front of me – a form of channeling I had never tried before. After grounding myself and protecting my energy, I asked to communicate with my spirit guides, and only for my highest good.

I expected a word or a sentence at the most, since that was common. Instead, I began receiving full paragraphs of clear and flowing messages – whispers that I could not explain, yet felt deeply guided. The first of those messages became the opening whisper in this book.

Through these teachings, I hope to offer comfort, insight, and understanding to anyone who feels called to read them. My guides and I ask only that you keep an open mind – take what resonates with you, and gently release what does not.

Happy journeying! We are definitely on a wild adventure.

Sincerely,

Kevin Wiczer & the Guides

Visit: www.GetKevInsight.com

WHAT YOU ARE ABOUT TO READ

Automatic writing, also called psychography, is the practice of producing written words without conscious thought, as if guided by a subconscious force, spirit, or external entity, often involving a trance-like or meditative state to bypass the analytical mind and access deeper insights.

On March 14, 2025, during recovery from back surgery, Kevin Wiczer began experiencing a series of these episodes.

Confined to physical stillness and spending extended periods in meditation, he noticed thoughts arriving that did not behave like ordinary imagination. They were not preceded by reflection, nor did they pause for clarification. The words came quickly, often faster than conscious thought could organize. Using his phone, Kevin typed continuously as the messages arrived.

There was no outline. No revision. No time to question meaning or intent. The priority was simply to record. The sessions did not feel theatrical or dramatic. There were no voices, visions, or trance rituals. The process was quiet, internal, and remarkably consistent. Once the messages began, they unfolded with their own structure.

At times, the information addressed subjects Kevin had not consciously considered. At other times, it challenged assumptions he already held. Patterns emerged gradually, often only becoming noticeable when messages were reviewed later.

The final transmission was received on December 24th, 2025; nine months after the transmissions first began. After the final message was received, no messages to be written down came through up until the publication of this book. Things went silent until the vocal channeling began.

Each transmission has been preserved exactly as it was received. No wording has been altered. Phrasing remains intact. The purpose of this book is not to persuade, convert, or explain away the experience. It is not a doctrine, a belief system, or a set of instructions. It is a record.

Whether these messages originate from the subconscious mind, an intuitive state, collective consciousness, spiritual intelligence, or something else entirely is left to the reader to determine. The only claim made here is that these words were not consciously authored in the traditional sense.

What follows is an unfiltered archive of the transmissions that came through those nine months in 2025. Read slowly. Notice what resonates. Question what does not. You are not required to believe anything. But you are invited to observe. The messages did not ask to be believed. They only asked to be read.

These are whispers from the infinite.

KEVIN WICZER

Whispers from the Infinite:

CHANNELED MESSAGES FROM

THE ETERNAL SOURCE

WHISPER I:

For Kevin

March 14th, 2025

"This is your guides explaining to you what you need to do next on your path. Meditation is key; that is the most important thing to remember. It is your tool to use when you feel lost and do not know what to do or where to go.

We are always here and we are always guiding you on your path even when you feel we are not there. Trust the process. You are exactly where you are meant to be at this exact moment. You do not have to fear anything because fear is a lower frequency that you can push to the side and ignore.

Everything is working out for your greater good. Even though you feel as though you are wandering you need to trust and believe that you are on the correct path. You are never wandering.

Nothing that has occurred in the past was for nothing. All has purpose. Theatre was necessary to get you where you are now. Those lessons you learned during that time were invaluable. You learned how to move forward on this new life path by learning from that chapter in your life. Believe.

You are currently surprised that you are writing all of this into your phone. You have been preparing for this moment for us to come through. Keep relaxed and breathe; all is well.

This message is to help you realize that you are not lost, you are not hopeless, you are not to be afraid. We have watched over you for so many lifetimes and we have guided you through these types of situations before. You have always had free will to do as you choose and we have always made sure that you have fulfilled your soul's destiny.

Know that you will help many people and that people will come to you more and more in the future. You have an inner knowing. You are continually growing. You have only just begun this new adventure and you will see how all the pieces of the puzzle will lay down perfectly as you press each piece into place.

Puzzles are challenging but they are necessary. They keep you alert and keep you moving. If you were given all the answers, what lessons would you be learning? You need to go through the process. You are not stuck. You are not confused. You do not have anything to worry about. We have protected you for a reason and you will discover what that reason is as the journey unfolds.

You continuously go to the tarot cards asking the same questions when we have already provided the answers to you before. Do you not believe what we are telling you? Do you think we are trying to make your life more difficult? The answer is, 'no'. We would never do that because of our unconditional love for you.

Just because you have had to learn some very challenging lessons in this lifetime does not mean we were not there. You needed to go through everything so that you could learn and grow and learn to live better than before. Challenges have purpose.

You have seen what losing everything – your home, your marriage, your dogs, your theatre career, your lifestyle, your pride – has done *for* you within the last few years. You gained so much more than you lost. You gained so much important knowledge about yourself that has taken you to this very moment now. You have had to trust that everything will work out, and it all has.

You have a stronger bond with your family and friends, you met Armando, you want to buy a home together. You and Armando are together in this part of your life because you would not have been able to truly appreciate and love each other without going through the challenging relationships you had before.

Now you know what true love feels like. You understand selflessness. You understand how your past illnesses had to teach you other lessons. You were never meant to die from those cancers you had, but you were meant to learn from them. The moment your time comes you will understand. That is the process.

That is the experience you have chosen. You are using your talents to channel us now and write down what you are hearing. That is because you have risen your frequency to a level where we can better communicate with you. These are not your thoughts. You need to trust that you are not making this up in your mind because you are not.

Nothing is a coincidence nothing is by chance. Now we ask you to share this message with others. We send you so much love as always, brave one. Thank you for listening."

WHISPER II:

Our Connection

March 16th, 2025

"We have something to share with people. Something you can share today. We are here to help you in any way possible, but please know that we will only step in if you ask us for help. If you do not ask us for help, we will leave you alone.

We are always sending you messages as not every thought you have is your own, but you need to know that you have access to us one hundred percent of the time and one hundred percent of every day. You are not alone in your journey. We are there with you always, but you cannot see us or feel us because of the different frequency of energy that flows.

We have watched you through your hardest times and we have watched you fall in love. These are beautiful moments in your life whether you are going through challenging times or incredible times. Positive or negative events are wonderful regardless because you are here to learn. Your soul cannot grow without learning. So, the loving times and the hard times are equally as important to experience.

Soul contracts are created by you with the assistance of us and your council. These decisions were made so that you could achieve the highest forms of learning to achieve the highest growth. Without these experiences, there would be no need to incarnate. It is also your choice how many times you wish to return, but those who return more often are the ones who are growing at a faster rate.

It is said that there are old souls and young souls. You talk of old and young souls often. However, the truth is that there are no old souls or young souls. The difference you feel and see within people who you feel are old and young souls is that the ones you feel are older souls are ones who have incarnated more often than those who have not. Those who have learned more often in a long period than others.

Those who have experienced more over the course of your lives than others. That is the difference. As we have stated earlier, you have a choice to come back as often as you wish. So, that is a choice. The door is always open to you to walk through. But what is also happening is that you are living all of your lives at the same time.

If you picture a jukebox full of records in a straight line, now turn those records into a stack that is vertical. Your soul is simply focusing on this one moment. This one blip of your existence. So, as you are living this life now, you are also living other lives at the same time. Time is not linear as it feels to you in your human body. To you time is linear and moves in a straight line. Things happen one after the other in a sequence of events that move forward in your mind.

However, time is not linear in the spirit realm. Time is not the same. These are things we wish for you to know at this time. Know that you are doing amazing things even when you feel you are not doing anything at all. Know that you are exactly where you are supposed to be right now and that you are not floundering. You are considered a hero in the spirit realm.

Why do we consider you humans as heroes? Because you chose to come back to learn the most difficult lessons in the universe. These are the lessons you cannot learn anywhere else due to the lower frequency you live in. This place you live is full of so many different energy frequencies that it can be extremely complicated to navigate through. Yet, you are navigating through it.

You are taking the most difficult challenges that others would not survive and instead you are thriving. It takes a considerable amount of courage to come to this dimension you are in and learn the most difficult lessons. That is why you have an entire team with you at all times that you are able to access at any moment just by asking us to step in and help.

If you need angels of a certain kind, ask for it out loud. Angels like it when you speak to them aloud. When we

say to call on your angels of a certain kind, we mean just that. When Kevin was going through his surgery, he asked, as many had asked, for angels who are knowing of surgical matters to assist in the operating room. Kevin called on the angels of surgery. There are angels who are experts in all different areas. All you need to do is be specific of the angels you wish to help you at that moment.

As we said before, life in this dimension is not easy and it is not meant to be easy. Just know that you are doing it and you are always applauded and celebrated. Your ancestors are proud of you as well as they continue to watch you throughout your short time on earth and as they decide when they want to return for another go around to learn, to grow, to love as you are doing at this very moment. Know that we love you unconditionally, and we are always by your side.

If you would like to connect with us, we suggest raising your frequency to the most positive it can be. You can do this by removing toxicity from your life or those who bring you down or cause you issues.

We also suggest meditation. During meditation, once you clear your mind, you may hear thoughts pop into your head that are not your own. You may see an image of something that we put in your head. You may smell something for a moment that is familiar. We communicate in many different ways to show you we are with you. If you see numbers all the time. We are showing you that we are there. We are sending you so much love, so much light, and so much support. Know that we are always cheering you on. Thank you for listening."

WHISPER III:

Challenging Moments

March 18th, 2025

"A question we received was why people must go through so much sadness and turmoil in their lifetime? We wanted to answer your question for you as that is a question that is often asked of us. People have asked this question forever. Life is meant to be challenging.

Please understand that the sad moments in your lives are not coincidental. They are designed by you, from you, for you. You are a soul that is so much bigger than your human self. Your human body is in your soul. Your soul is not in your body. Your soul is much larger than your human body. This is important to understand because your soul is in control of your experience the whole time as we assist in what your soul is asking for experience wise.

Imagine this life as a video game. You like video games because each video game provides you with a certain experience. Notice how most video games frustrate you because they are challenging at times. This is very similar to how lifetimes work. Your soul chooses a certain experience they would like to have, and then you plug into the experience you have chosen, and then it begins.

Now, life is not a game, but that is just a very simple way of explaining the experience to you without getting complicated. Soul contracts are drawn up by you with our guidance and expertise. As you live your lives, you are given experiences to help you for your next lifetime full of more experiences.

It is like the video game reference again. In order to get to level two you must get through level one. And you cannot get to level twenty if you have not gone through all the other levels first. Some souls have tried to take on too much during a lifetime when they were not ready for it yet. As though you are playing a video game and you warp from level two to level twenty and you were not ready. You did not have the experiences and knowledge that you needed to understand fully the difficulty of level twenty.

So, as we advise souls not to take on too much, in the end, it is the soul's decision what they wish to take on. We cannot stop a soul from warping from level two to twenty. At those moments, you may see suicide occur. Now, we understand that suicide is a very triggering subject, so we will not stay on the subject for long. But this is to help you understand that souls sometimes take on too much.

However, when souls listen to our guidance as they prepare to incarnate on this planet once again, you will notice that life is challenging, sometimes extremely challenging, but is still manageable.

We will take Kevin's life as an example again since he is channeling us at the moment. Kevin's higher self does not mind us using him as an example, in fact, it was their idea.

Kevin has been 'through it' as some of you would say. Kevin has been through surgeries, challenging times with relationships, had lost everything he hoped for in his life, has had cancer three times, has hit rock bottom to spark the beginning of his spiritual enlightenment journey.

However, through it all, he has managed to come out of it stronger. Now, Kevin has been around the block as a soul many, many times before. He has been preparing for this lifetime from the very beginning when he made the choice to begin these Earthly journeys. Is this his last lifetime on Earth? That will be Kevin's higher self's choice, but this is his lifetime of final completion. It is his legacy lifetime, where he must now share and leave behind this information to help the world remember.

For the human mind, it can sound daunting imagining coming back lifetime after lifetime, challenge after challenge. When you have been through a lot, it is hard to imagine that you have to come back again and do it all over with new lessons and new challenges.

But souls love every minute of it. Do you understand? Souls love playing 'video games.' Because these video games are exciting and they help souls to learn and grow. They help souls to 'level up,' as Kevin would say.

Your soul is going through its own set of challenges that were chosen by you and for you. You are simply playing out everything you have designed for this lifetime. Everything has a reason. Everything has a purpose and meaning. Nothing is coincidence.

Back to sadness and turmoil and all that is painful in life. Take yourself out of the situations you have gone through in the past. Step back. Take a closer look as an observer rather than the player itself. What were you meant to learn from these experiences? How have those past or current experiences helped to get you where you are today?

Kevin is currently wondering when this writing session will end. He is thinking it is too long, but we will end momentarily. See? We too have a sense of humor.

Look back to those experiences and realize that without those events, you would not be where you are right now. We will go back to the puzzle idea. Without all the pieces to the puzzle, you cannot have a full puzzle. Every moment in your life is a puzzle piece. That makes every moment in your life significant. Everything is happening for a reason and everything is happening for you, by you, from outside of this dimension.

We are always here for you. Always watching, and always guiding. Think of us as the manual to the challenging video game. We are here when you get to the most difficult parts. But if you do not pick up the manual and ask for help, you may find yourself stuck in a certain part of the simulation.

Remember to always ask for help. Be specific on how we can be of assistance, and we will meet you halfway to help you as long as you meet us halfway and do the work as well. You will find that you will get the answers you need, and you will get through the challenging parts.

We hope that this helps you in understanding why people go through hard and challenging times in their lives. And we hope we have answered the question to your satisfaction. We are always sending you love. Thank you for listening."

WHISPER IV:

The Need for Humor

March 20th, 2025

"There is something we would like to say. It is about humor. Humor is such a powerful thing. There is much humor all around you. Humor is a beautiful type of positive energy. People use it to raise their energy frequency. Try it sometime. When you are sick or you are angry, try watching something funny and you will notice a shift in your consciousness. You will feel a lightness within you.

This works in every situation. If you take funerals. Human beings are often very sad at these occasions, but you will notice that people will begin to tell funny stories so they are able to release the negative energy that is being held from within them. Humor gives you the opportunity to come back to a neutral state.

It takes you out of the negative frequency you are being enveloped in, and it is giving you the opportunity to raise that frequency for your own good. Without humor, human beings would not be able to survive. This is not just for the human species, but all species within the universe.

There are beings all over the universe that use humor as protection against negative energy. Humor, being the very high frequency that it is, is not only in what you would consider 'living' beings, but also in spirit. Yes, you are a 'human being,' but you also double as a spiritual being as well. You are both. However, you are always a spiritual being and only a human being for short moments in space and time. In the spirit realm, we use humor constantly.

For example, we will use Kevin again, since Kevin has raised his frequency and is able to hear us and channel us more, he will sometimes notice hearing our laughter when something funny occurs as we watch. We love humor. We love everything that is of positive energy. Kevin gets a kick out of it when he can hear our laughter as well.

We are always ready for a good joke, and sometimes we will pop a thought or picture into his mind that will make him laugh out of nowhere. We do the same to you. Have you ever just been sitting around either watching television or at work and suddenly a thought, memory, or picture of something hilarious pops into your head and you start laughing out of nowhere? That is not a coincidence. We are just trying to get you to 'lighten up' in that moment. And by lighten up, we mean that in the literal sense.

Positive energy is very light in density where negative energy is very heavy and dense or as Kevin likes to call it 'sludgy.' There are no negative frequencies in this dimension we are in. We are incapable of lowering our energy to that low of frequency, so that is why in order to communicate with us well, you need to raise your frequency as high as you possibly can, and we will reach as far as we can to meet you halfway and begin the communication. Humor is one of the most precious energies in the universe and beyond.

If you are ill, we encourage you to watch hours and hours of hilarious comedy that uplifts you. Stay away from movies, music, and podcasts that make you sad or infuriate you or scare you. Sadness, anger, and fear are low frequencies. These energies will actually make you sicker longer. If you are in a neutral environment and you are ill, the illness will last for an average amount of time. The choice is yours.

Remember that everything has an energy frequency attached to it. Everything, everyone, everywhere. So, since that is the case, you must know and understand the Law of Attraction. What energy you give out to the universe the universe will give back to you. This is not out of punishment or judgement because there is no punishment or judgement, but because the universe is giving you the experience you are asking for.

That is why all of your thoughts, your words you speak, and the actions you take are very important. Attached to each of those is energy, and the universe will receive it and send it back to you in return. So, if you are angry at someone and it has really gotten to you, it will come back to you in other negative ways. Do you notice when you are in a negative state of mind, negative things begin to happen around you? Your car does not work, or you are caught behind slow vehicles, or something breaks down in your home out of nowhere and you need to replace it or suddenly you have unexpected bills to pay, etc.

These are not coincidences as there are no coincidences in this universe. Everything is happening for a reason energetically. We hope that that makes sense. So be very mindful of this.

Human beings are very addicted to the news. Not only is the news created to produce negative reactions and frequencies, but it has also become an addiction. Addictions of all kinds are very low energy frequencies. Be very careful about this as it will affect your personal life in more ways than one.

It is one thing to be quickly informed about something and then you move on about your day bringing positive energy wherever you go, and it is another to be immersed in the drama and toxicity of the news where you are posting angry messages, threatening others, and living in a life of misery.

The Law of Attraction does not discriminate. Even if you are fighting for a cause, you are passionate about, if you are not doing it in a positive way without aggression or anger, it will come back to you, affecting your personal life in some way. You do not deserve that as life is already challenging enough as it is. There is no reason to make your life more difficult.

Now for some people reading this, you will start to get defensive, but there is no reason to. You cannot stop energy from flowing and it will continue to flow regardless of how you feel about what we have said. Remember to stay in a positive energy frequency as much as possible. You are not doing it for others around you; you are doing it for yourself.

You cannot control other people's energy; you can only control your own. There is comfort knowing you have that type of power within you. Use that power. It seems we have wandered from humor to other subjects, but we always have so much to say and to share.

We hope that this message helps to make your life even a little bit easier. There is power in understanding. There is power in knowledge. We want you to have the best experience possible, and we will always do what we can to help and guide.

As always, we are sending you so much love and light. And as you read this message, we hope that you felt our positive and healing energy flowing through you. And as for humor, we hope you laugh a bit today. Smile a bit today. And love. We love you dearly, our friends. Thank you for listening."

WHISPER V:

Your Soul

March 21ˢᵗ, 2025

"We are here to talk through Kevin again with another interesting subject. We are all here to help each other. We are all connected. You are a part of a soul group that travels from lifetime to lifetime to offer each other a multitude of different experiences.

Your soul group was chosen at the beginning when you were created. There are more soul groups than you could ever imagine. For instance, you have or had a mother or father. In another lifetime they were something else in relation to you. Could be your sister or your best friend or someone who hurt you in another life. It is whatever you agreed upon with your soul group before returning to live that life.

As a soul you do not identify as any sex. You are a spiritual being without gender. Soul contracts are created by you, your guides, your council, but while other souls in your soul group are planning their return as well, everyone's stories are carefully interwoven so that everyone involved learns the lessons they needed to learn in their time on earth as well. This is an agreement amongst you.

While life is happening for you, everything just seems to fit in place. You have had moments where you feel you have known certain people all of your life. They seem so familiar. Because you have known them for many of your lifetimes. You have been through more together than you will ever know. That is why you connect with certain people so intensely and why you do not connect with others.

We have mentioned video games as an example in a past channeling session, and instead we are going to use an example of a theatrical production. As a group, with your soul group, your spirit guides, your light council, all together create a soul contract that is very much like writing a play together. You have the stories, the sub plots, you have the characters and all of their characteristics, and you have how everyone is connected. Think of this as an outline. You finish the script which is full of many moments where you are able to improvise also known as free will. But you will always get to your main plot points.

We are your stage managers. We make sure you are following the script, however, if you get too far off track with improvisation, it is our job to bring you back to the play that was written. Sometimes that is harder to do than others because some people really enjoy going far, far, far off script, so we need to take some drastic measures to insure you come back to follow your plot lines.

If you find that we are putting obstacle after obstacle in your way, and you do not understand why everything is not working out for you at that moment, it is because you have deviated too much from your plot line, and we need you to get back on track. This is not a punishment and we do not judge you. We simply need you to follow the script you have written so that you learn the lessons you were meant to learn.

When you are on the correct course, you will find that doors open up for you a bit easier. It still takes hard work, and there are always challenges, but you will find that it is not impossible. Challenges are important in life. You grow the most through the most difficult moments. But remember, if you keep bumping into wall after wall and you cannot get through, it means you need to turn around and get back on track.

When you really focus on getting back on your path, you will find it is more about letting go of control. But the first important part is realizing that you are improvising too much and that you have deviated too much from the text. For some, that is very difficult for them to admit because they wish to be going in another direction instead. But it is important to have that talk with yourself and figure it out. That is part of the journey.

Meditation also helps to ground yourself and have a clear head. This message is to show you that you are all connected for a reason. There's purpose in everything. Some

beings in your soul group are there to play a smaller role, and others are meant to be key players. Everything has purpose. Believe. And through everything that happens, the show must go on.

Here is a question for contemplation: what positive lessons do you think you were meant to learn so far? Why do you think your higher-self chose this experience at this moment? These are questions that are always interesting to ponder. We hope this message helped in some way, and as always, we are sending our love and light to you!"

WHISPER VI:

Soul Groups

March 23rd, 2025

"We are back to discuss a topic that was asked of us from Kevin's mother. Her higher-self has allowed us to mention her as she asked the question. She wanted to know more about soul groups. This is a very interesting topic that we would love to speak to because this can be very difficult to understand without images, so we have a few images that will help to explain.

First, we will dive into what a soul group is. At the time of creation, we (as in all of us, everyone, everywhere, and everything) became an extension of the Divine Creator. You can call it God, Source, Mother Father God, the Creator, the Divine, it really does not matter what you call it. It is everything. It is unconditional love. It is all of us as we are all extensions of it; fractals.

We have mentioned the sweater analogy before. We are each a thread in a beautiful sweater of light. We are all light as well. Without one piece of beautiful thread, the entire sweater would unravel. That makes each of us extremely important. Without one of us, the entire universe would unravel. That is how powerful you are. You may not feel that way because as human beings you sometimes feel rather small and insignificant at times, but you have no idea how untrue that is.

You are a divine piece of the puzzle of the universe. You are so much more than your tiny vessel that you call your human body. That is the first part of understanding. Before you can understand soul groups, you must understand the soul first and how we are all connected.

Now, for soul groups. When everything was created, we were placed into sections or groupings. Think of a quilt instead if that helps even more. When all was created, it became a large, ever expanding quilt (expanding because all of us are continually growing, and as we are growing, so is the Creator, hence why we must learn what we can so that we can grow in size and help the expansion of Source as we are extensions of it), so let us go back to the quilt analogy.

As we were created, we were immediately grouped like the sections of a quilt. We were all still connected, but we all had our own group of souls that you would continue to learn and grow with to help the expansion. But each soul group is connected.

Now it begins to get more complicated than that, so without trying to make your heads explode, we will try to make this as simple as we can. Kevin's mother understood what soul groups were, but she could not understand how large a soul group could be.

For example, is everyone you know or have met in your life a part of your soul group? But what about those people in your life that you know such as your best friend? Do they have their own soul group too? They have other significant people in their own lives who you have never met before. If your best friend is a part of your soul group, are they a part of another soul group as well? Or are those people you do not know also in your soul group?

Let us break this down as simply as we can with the image of the Olympic emblem. Think of it this way, everyone you know in your own life who plays a significant part or even a small part, is part of your own individual soul group. So, that would be one circle of the Olympic emblem. Now notice another circle. Let us say that it is your best friend's circle. They have their own soul group of people you have never met before, but they are significant to your best friend, however, both of your circles are interconnected.

Two different soul groups but still connected. Now look at the Olympic emblem to understand what we mean. All soul groups are connected because everyone and everything in the universe is connected. We are all a part of the Creator. Now instead of only five rings in the emblem, think about more rings than you could ever imagine. We are all linked together. That is how we would like to explain soul groups and how you are all connected.

Does this make sense? We hope that it does as it gets even more complex and more complicated than that, but hopefully that explanation gives you a general idea of how everything works. We loved that question and are always happy to explain in a way that is as understandable as possible. Sometimes images are the best way to describe how something works.

And as always, we are so happy to be able to give you information to help you to learn and understand, mostly so that you can remember who you truly are as a divine being of light and love. We are sending you so much love and light. Thank you for this opportunity to speak to you, and thank you for listening."

WHISPER VII:

Trust the Process

March 24, 2025

"We have something to say, and we wanted to share it with you. It is about trusting the process. That what you are hearing in your minds is not something you are making up. We place many messages in your minds to help guide you in the right direction. Not only actual thoughts but numbers, symbols, animals, songs on the radio, etc. We have many different ways to communicate. It just happens to be what you need most at any given time.

Here is a message from us to you. Keep positive energy flowing through you at all times. Love everyone but first begin with loving yourself. Try not to judge others who are on similar or even different paths than you. Every experience is custom made by each of you, so their experience is their experience for a reason that can only be known or understood by them.

You as well as everyone around you have chosen to come back at this time because it is an incredible moment of spiritual history on earth. The awakening of the entire planet is slowly beginning. We bring this up as this was a big topic of conversation with Kevin's family yesterday. We listen all the time, see?

Some of you will see the beginnings of it, and others will see much more, but it is happening at a rapid pace as your linear time moves forward. More and more people are awakening each day. They are seeing the cracks in broken systems of religion, government, healthcare, etc. And as people see the cracks as a collective, changes will be made. And eventually when the entire world awakens, this planet will move from a 3D world and it will upgrade to 4D consciousness, and eventually 5D consciousness.

That is because the frequency of the entire planet will rise. Now, that will take hundreds of years, but you are witnessing the beginning, and that is one of the most exciting and thrilling times to be incarnated.

There is power in numbers. If the whole world or even most of the world manifested beautiful things together in the name of love and compassion, everything in life and all that surrounds you would change. It would instantly be a different earth. A different place. Unrecognizable to you but in the most beautiful ways.

You are seeing the start. The beginning is history in the making that you are a part of. You are the start. You are the ones who are beginning to change the frequency of this planet. Without you, this new beginning would not have occurred. Every day more and more cracks in powerful systems are being seen by many people, and more and more people are wanting big changes. That will come in time. Believe and trust the process.

Now, let us move onto a more fun subject, shall we? Let us talk about birthdays because it is Kevin's birthday today in human form. It is not only celebrated on earth but also celebrated in the spirit realm. Why should it be celebrated? Because what you decided to do and accomplish on earth is very heroic. It is not easy to make the decision to return to earth and learn such difficult lessons. It is true that your higher self loves every moment of it, but a lot of energy is used on all ends.

There are people on earth who wish to not celebrate birthdays or it makes them sad because their physical bodies are a year older. You are sad that you are not as young as you were. Does it help you to know that you are ancient in terms of your soul? Ancient. You have been around from the beginning of creation. Yes, that ancient.

So, no need to worry no matter what age your physical bodies are turning. When you incarnate again, you will be young again for a short time, just in a different vessel. So, no need to fret and go ahead and celebrate this beautiful day where you decided to return to earth and accomplish your very important heroic journey. We celebrate it with you because the journey you are on is not easy.

It is 3:47am and Kevin is tired and would like to go back to sleep, but he has the day off tomorrow and still recovering from his back surgery so he can sleep in for his birthday. See? More humor.

With that note, we will end this session. But we will finish by saying: celebrate yourself because you have no idea what experiences you have been through to get where you are today. Whether you have decided to return more often than others or not. You are old. We are all old.

Now celebrate your special day of coming to earth and being heroic with pride. You deserve it, and you have earned it. In fact, you should celebrate it every day of your life. So, turn 43 or 67 or 94. Trust us when we say that sounds very young to us.

Now, eat some cake, because we cannot. But we enjoy watching you celebrate yourself. Splurging a little to bring yourself joy is not a bad thing. Now we will end this session so Kevin may go back to sleep. We send you love and light as always and thank you for listening."

WHISPER VIII:

A Thought on Religion

March 25th, 2025

"Hello, friends. We would like to speak to you all about religion. We know many human beings have very strong ideas and thoughts about religion, and we wanted to speak on it today. Religion has been an interesting point of conversation for thousands and thousands of years.

There are those who seem to believe their religion is the most important or the better of all religions. They think their own religion reigns supreme above the rest. This has not only caused conflict, but it has caused many wars, millions upon millions of deaths, and so much turmoil on your precious planet.

How sad is it that something that was meant to bring people together is the same thing that has caused and continues to cause so much hatred, separation, and upset. Now yes, it is true that those who have been affected by these awful times had asked to be a part of these experiences as higher selves before coming to earth to live their lives. They sacrificed and continue to sacrifice themselves in such a heroic way to show how horrendous and horrible people can treat each other for no other reason other than they are different than someone else. Those brave souls have sacrificed themselves to show those cracks in the systems. Now that time has passed, people are seeing that this is wrong.

How has it taken this long to recognize? Why has it taken so long to see that your differences are beautiful and not something to destroy each other over? Now, it is true that these souls came down here to "take one for the team" as you say. They were heroes who needed to be a part of the realization era. The era where people saw that that behavior was barbaric and horrific.

However, the realization era is still happening. You are slowly coming to its closure. It has taken this long for people to start waking up. But out of the whole world, only a small percentage really understand this. There are still so many that would rather hate than love. It is because living in negative frequencies can be very addictive. There is something about the toxicity and drama and the hierarchy humans have created for themselves that is like being on an addictive substance.

What is toxicity? It is in the name itself. Toxic. Something that is toxic is generally considered unhealthy and dangerous. This is why toxic people stay in that low density. Toxic energy is created by humans. It is a human creation, and has been around for many, many thousands of years, they just never called it that.

For some, hatred and anger are exciting and pleasurable in a way. Even those who live in fear and enjoy trying to rile others up to feel the same way is exciting and a different type of toxicity. This is important while trying to explain religion and what religion has done to the human species.

Let us explain. There have been many masters who have ascended, who no longer have the need to return to live again in human form. A few examples on earth would be Buddha, Jesus, Babaji, Yogananda, various people who people consider saints, those who have done miraculous things, etc. There are many, many ascended masters. Not only are there ascended masters from earth, but there are ascended masters from all walks of life all over the universe and other dimensions.

Now, these masters taught much of the same teachings such as love, compassion, respect, finding your bliss. All of which are positive frequencies. That is because the veil between the human realm and the spirit realm was nonexistent for them. They lived in both realms at the same time. The more you learn and grow and understand , the thinner and thinner the veil becomes. Hence why souls incarnate as much as they do. We hope that makes sense.

However, human beings of lower frequencies have taken those beautiful teachings, and they have purposefully 'fixed' them for their own benefit. They switched and twisted words around to control people and have power over them.

Human beings created Hell or a place of doom for those who did not comply and follow the powerful humans' rules. It is all about the hierarchy; who is at the top, and who is at the bottom? You can only have power over those who are afraid. Those who live in fear are the easiest to be controlled.

Now, let us tell you how we feel about your religions of the world. It is not that we do not approve that there are religions. It is that there are so many negative, low frequency teachings that are taught. Teachings that 'you must follow us or else –' There is still so much exclusion. So much hate. So much anger. So much fear. Even down to what you eat.

We will take Catholicism for a moment because that is how Kevin was brought up. If you eat meat on Friday, what will happen to you? Nothing. If you choose not to eat meat because you are choosing to be vegetarian, that is your choice. But to not eat meat on a Friday because you will be doomed to a fiery pit with torturous demons if you do is not correct. This is a small way to control. It is only *your* business what you choose to eat or choose not to eat.

They have many people so controlled that religious wars are still occurring today. Where is the love in that? Where is the comradery? Where is the compassion for other precious life? As you can see, for many humans, there is still so much that needs to be learned. And now you see why reincarnation is so necessary. The learning process must continue. You must master both high and low frequency dimensions for your soul to fully ascend.

We see religions or those with no religion as a large hand with many fingers. Where do the individual fingers all connect to? The palm. This means that all religions or no religion or not believing in anything at all, all lead to the same place. It does not matter what you believe or what you do not believe. Just live with love in your heart for yourself and for others, help those people who are in need when you are able because we are all connected, and find your happiness and fulfillment. Have those experiences.

It is really that simple. We do not mind religion fully because there are positive teachings mixed in. So, if you want to be a part of a religion, take the good and positive teachings and discard the negative ones. Anything low frequency does not resonate with us. Only the highest frequencies.

We will get into life reviews another time because we are reading certain minds who are wondering about that. 'If there is no Hell, where do the really negative and destructive and harmful people go?' That is a large, complex topic for another time.

In the meantime: live, love, learn, and grow. Do not hurt others, love them. Do not condemn others, include them. When we hurt others, we hurt ourselves because we are all one. We hope that all of this makes sense to you. We are sending all of you so much love and light. And we hope that this has helped you in some way. We thank you for listening."

WHISPER IX:

The Transition

March 26th, 2025

"Hello, dear friends, we wanted to speak on a subject that many of you have been asking about in your minds for some time. Now, a lot of you may already know this, but this is for those who may still be curious or need more of an explanation, or, even perhaps, validation.

This subject is about what happens after you transition from your human body to the spirit realm and this topic will also include the life review process. We hope that this discussion will clear up some questions you may have. So 'buckle up' as you humans like to say.

Let us first discuss what happens when you transition. There is so much fear around the word 'death.' We are not the biggest fans of that word because it sounds so final, and that is further from the truth. Though 'death' can also mean the end of one big chapter and the beginning of another; we like that description much better. We would rather think of 'death' in that way. But for our sake and yours, we will use the word 'transition.'

Human beings are often afraid of transitioning over because they do not know what happens. The truth is that one to five minutes before your body shuts down like a machine, you have already left your body and transitioned. It is because you have left your physical body that your vessel shuts down. It is like pulling the plug on a machine. Without electricity, the machine might work for a moment, but then it slowly stops. Same concept.

Some transition quicker depending on the circumstances such as major accidents or something of that nature where the soul leaves much more abruptly. In fact, it happens so easily and simply that most who transition over often have the moment of 'that was it? That was what I was so worried about my whole lifetime?'

We hope that knowing this information relaxes you. Leaving your body is something your soul is so used to because you have been doing it over and over again for many, many lifetimes. With the help of some angels, ancestors, or even on your own depending on soul mastery, you simply remember how to do it depending on how often you have reincarnated. So, do not fret about transitioning. It is a 'piece of cake' as you say. Now, do not live your life in fear, but do not be reckless either, life is very precious.

We will continue. You have now transitioned. Some go through a tunnel, some feel like they are flying through the universe, some feel like they are walking through a forest. Everyone has a different experience depending on what you want or hope to happen. Again, you are manifesting the experience at all times. It does not matter how your soul chooses to get to our realm; it happens very quickly. Practically instantaneously.

When you arrive, you will have a sense of remembering where you are; though the 'amnesia' you had agreed to have before your incarnation wears off slowly. Again, where you are looks different for everyone as you are manifesting the experience. Some are in a beautiful garden, some see large structures like buildings, some are in the void, seeing nothing around them but hear, feel, and even smell unconditional love and safety.

Regardless of what you manifest at that time, we, your guides, will meet up with you and make sure your transition process goes smoothly. Do not worry, you will remember us very well once we reconnect. We always love seeing you. After discussing how you thought your life went and all the lessons you may have learned, it is time for your life review. This is also an experience that is specific to you.

No life review experience is the same as another. Some see their review like they are a part of a movie; some see a row of screens; some look into a pond. It is different for everyone depending on how you want it to be. There is one thing that is the same for all life reviews. That is for that moment you are given the opportunity (not by choice) to feel negative frequencies again such as pain and hurt.

We call it an opportunity because otherwise, you do not feel pain or negative energy when you are home, only positive energy. The highest frequencies. It may not seem like it, but that is a gift.

During this process, you go through your entire life, stopping at significant moments where you may have made someone incredibly happy or the opposite. The difference is that you feel how the other person felt at that time.

We will give you a few examples. If you brought joy to someone else, you will feel that person's overwhelming joy in that moment. If you were not so nice to someone and hurt someone's feelings, you will feel that horrible hurt you made them feel. If you were violent with someone, you will feel the exact physical pain that you inflicted upon them from the moment it began to the moment it ended.

Now we will get to what some had wondered about in cases of people who, we will sensitively say, 'off' others. Those souls feel all the pain and suffering from the moment it began to the moment it ended. Now, because there is no Hell, we suppose that process above certainly may sound something like it. However, we do not see it that way, please understand. We do not judge you and we do not punish.

Remember how we say that life is a learning experience? Consider your life review as your final exam. It is the time when you learn the most from how you lived in physical form. Does that make sense? When you feel that pain and suffering and hurt you may have caused others, you are less likely as a soul to want to have that experience again. You have learned and have grown.

Now if you take someone who, for example, has physically hurt millions of people, their life review takes 'a while', but because time does not exist in our realm, saying 'a while' is meaningless. However, those people who have hurt many must feel each of those individual soul's pain and suffering one after the other after the other. How long is 'a while'? It is too difficult to explain without making your head spin. We find easier explanations best.

Again, this is a learning experience not a punishment, but we can see how that would sound 'Hellish.' We do not consider it that way though. However, then we get into karma, and that is a completely different topic of conversation for another time.

Let us continue. Once the life review is over, it is time to cleanse your soul of all the negative energy that may be connected or 'sticking' to you. The 'sludge' Kevin likes to call it. This happens in various ways through energy with the help of our beautiful light friends who assist us in this cleansing. After your soul has all the 'sludge' removed, you will feel the incredible lightness that we feel always. You are home. Joined together with your soul groups again. Such a beautiful moment.

This post was meant to be about the transition process and life review than anything else, so we will stop there for now as this has gotten pretty lengthy and you have lives to live.

We hope what we have said today makes sense, and we hope that it has given you comfort, and validated or helped you in some way. As always, we send you love and light, and thank you for listening."

WHISPER X:

Karma

March 27th, 2025

"Hello, have you missed us? We love you all very much. We are back to talk through Kevin as he is up and still recovering from a painful back surgery. These sessions not only help others, but they also help him.

Positive energy is healing. As we speak through him, he often notices a reduction of pain that he is experiencing. This is not a coincidence. Healing is a process, but we will always do what we can to help. We are so glad that these messages that we have given have helped so many people and will continue to help so many.

We cannot tell you everything as there are many things that you will need to figure out on your own because it is a part of your journey here. We cannot interfere with your life path because it was chosen by you and it is a path that must be followed. However, the trick is that we cannot tell you what that life path is because there is a lot of learning that must be done on your own before you can fully and truly begin your journey.

Just know that those who feel you are wandering are not actually wandering at all. You are exactly where you are meant to be at this exact moment in time. So, as much as it can feel lonely or frustrating or scary, take a pause, take a moment to ground yourself through meditative practices. We encourage everyone to do this.

Kevin continues to say that it is difficult for him to meditate while he is feeling the intense aching and throbbing pain from his surgery. But we will say that that is exactly *when* he should be meditating. And we hope when he reads this back that he will consider it and change his mind as meditation can help inflammation and pain. He is saying 'okay, okay' as we just mentioned it. Very good.

We wanted to speak about karma today as we mentioned karma in the last message. What is karma? Energy that follows you is the easiest way to explain it. You have both positive and negative karma depending on how you treat others and live your life. Let us talk about positive karma first.

Positive karma occurs when you bring joy to others, when you are helping humanity in some way, when you do things out of the goodness of your heart without expecting something in return, when you help change someone's life for the better, when you help to shine your light on those who feel like they are in the dark. When you touch even one person's life, energy surrounding the event turns into a positive charge, and therefore becomes positive karma.

Energy cannot be created or destroyed, but the frequency of the energy can always be changed or shifted. All of your thoughts, actions, and words you speak have an energy charge or frequency attached to it. This includes the Law of Attraction, but when you are doing things for other people, it becomes karmic energy. Karmic energy follows you through not only your life now, but to your next lives.

We will go back to positive karma. The more you are selfless and help other people, bring joy to other people's lives, serve humanity in a beautiful way, that karmic energy follows you. Imagine a beautiful bubble of light that is surrounding you. This bubble of light follows you through your life and your lifetimes.

On the other hand, with positive karmic energy comes negative karmic energy. Negative karmic energy is exactly the opposite of helping those around you, but instead, harming those around you. Living selfishly and only for yourself and your own good, not caring for those people who are less fortunate than you, not learning the important lessons of life that help to treat people with love, kindness, respect, and compassion.

The energy surrounding you then has a negative charge and negative karma surrounds you instead. Think of the bubble of light turning into a dark cloud. This energy follows you as well. The more negative karmic energy you have, the more it grows and grows. The worse you treat humanity such as 'offing others' we will say sensitively, that negative karma is so great, it will be impossible to change that negative karma in one lifetime. This negative karma follows you into your next life or lives and will heavily affect you during that time. But let us say that if it is not as negative of a situation as was just mentioned, negative karma can be changed even within your lifetime now.

Let us explain. Positive energy, light, will always conquer the darkness. If you have a flashlight and you walk into a dark room, can you not see? Of course you can. Light is more powerful than darkness. This means that if you have negative karmic energy attached to you, and you decide to change your ways to serve humanity and love others and help people in beautiful ways, you have the ability to slowly change the karmic frequency that surrounds you.

Can you get rid of all of your negative karma? The answer is possibly. It really depends on how much negative karmic energy you have created. For example, the cloud reference. It depends on how large and thick the dark cloud is surrounding you. If you change your frequency to a more positive one, you may be able to change some of the energy, but not all. In this situation, that karmic energy will follow you into your next life or lives.

In your next life, if you continue to change the negative karma into positive karma, there is a chance that you will raise the frequency of the rest of the negative karmic energy, hence giving it a positive charge. Then you will be

surrounded by the bubble of light rather than the cloud. We hope that this makes sense to you.

Please understand, no one is perfect. Everyone on your planet makes mistakes. That is how you learn and grow. Sometimes your frustrations can get the better of you and you may lash out at another person or something of that nature.

It is true that this produces negative karmic energy, but if you are generally a person who is loving to others and compassionate to other people, and help others in need, that puff of dark cloud generated by the isolated incident will change frequency rather quickly.

Our advice to you is just to do your best to live with love and compassion for others as well as yourself. Treat others with respect and kindness. Bring joy to others and help those who are less fortunate when you are able. That is what we suggest.

In short, just do your best. As always, we are sending you love and light. Thank you for listening."

WHISPER XI:

Time Manipulation

April 1st, 2025

"Hello friends. We are back with another message through Kevin. This one is about your ability to manipulate time. Now it is true that you are unable to bend and stretch time exactly the way that we can or at the extent that we can, but you will notice that you do have the ability to manipulate time on your planet and you do not even recognize that you are doing it most of the time. Rather, you do it without even thinking about it.

Notice when you are having a frustrating or boring day, and the day, then, seems to move at a glacial pace. And when you are having the time of your life and you are at your happiest, time seems to move very quickly. This is not a coincidence.

You are able to manipulate time based on the energy that is surrounding you and within you. Remember that everything is energy and everything is connected energetically, and as human beings you are capable of manipulating it in different ways; just as you can manipulate energy and change it from negative to positive energy and vice versa in regard to the Law of Attraction we have been talking about before.

Frustration and boredom are negative energy frequencies, and since negative energy frequencies have a 'sludgy' feel to them, as Kevin calls it, you will feel time begin to drag behind and slow down. Almost as though your physical body is ahead of the actual time itself, but time is really being held back by energy. The energy you are feeling around you and the energy you are expelling has literally manipulated linear time to become slower.

Happiness and fun and humor are positive energy frequencies, and the more positive the energy you surround yourself with and is expelled from you, the lighter the energy becomes, thus making time move at a faster pace. This is why when you are out with your friends, you look at the time and hours have gone by in what felt like minutes. You have manipulated time.

Often when you are with others, and you are all expelling the same energy, the time will speed up or slow down as a collective because the energy force is even stronger when multiple people in the same group are expelling the same energy. Does that make sense? We hope that it does.

We are telling you this to prove, once again, how powerful you are and you do not even realize it. You are doing this subconsciously just as you are subconsciously sending out positive or negative energy out into the universe in regard to the Law of Attraction.

All of this is working together at the same time. Energy is constantly flowing from us to us and all around us. And being energy beings at your core, you can see how that is to your benefit. Now that you know, try noticing this time energy manipulation in the future. Test it out. You have already felt this before so this is nothing new, but perhaps you just were not aware that you are the one or ones manipulating time. That is very powerful. You are all much more powerful than you think as the human species. And there is always power in knowing and understanding.

If you are in a situation where time is being slowed down by negative energy, shift the negative energy into positive energy by doing something you enjoy and brings you happiness, you will notice time speed up. For example, at work, if you are having a bad day or you are bored and time is moving slowly, put on some upbeat, fun music you love or watch hilarious videos on your break. And as your mood shifts frequencies, you will notice time moving faster. Try it out and see for yourself.

So, you may not be able to bend and stretch time exactly the way that we can (though there are some who can with practice), you are certainly able to control the speed of time based on your surrounding energy, the energy frequency from within you, and the environment.

This is one of the 'cool' things, as you would say, that you are capable of. We love having these wonderful conversations with you. It always brings us so much joy to communicate in this manner. As always we send you love and light, and thank you for listening."

WHISPER XII:

War

April 2nd, 2025

"Hello, our old and dear friends. Today we wish to talk to you to discuss a very important and sensitive topic. This is about war on your planet. We first need to express that we do not judge you for your decisions that you make in your dimension. Judgement is something we do not do and have never done.

These are observations that we will make because we understand the cause. How are wars created? How have wars began for thousands and thousands of years on your planet. It comes down to money and power and greed. We need to examine each of these very low frequencies to understand how wars begin first.

Let us examine money. Money is a difficult thing because you all tell each other that you need it to survive. You see these individual pieces of paper or even just digitally on a screen, and the numbers of how much you have go up and down causing you more stress and anxiety. Money is the cause of much stress and anxiety on your planet. Without it, you feel you will lose everything. You have placed so much importance, stress, and anxiety into a piece of paper as a collective that these little pieces of paper have a powerful, negative hold over you and everyone you know.

However, in order for this piece of paper to have any sort of significance, everyone must agree that it does. You have all agreed as a collective around the world. So therefore, it now runs your lives in a negative way. You have placed an energy onto it that you put on a pedestal above your own power. These pieces of paper known as money are a negative energy frequency because it controls everything you do.

This is why we would never say to manifest money. You are giving your power away to an object rather than taking your power back. We tell you to manifest what you want in your life instead, a home, love, relationships, a career you are passionate about, etc. these are all beautiful frequencies. When you manifest these positive things, money will follow. But we digress.

Those who manifest money are never really happy once they receive it. Because once you get some money, you want more of it, and more of it. It is never enough. And rather than sharing money to help others in need once someone has an abundance of it, many keep it to themselves because again, there is never enough of it. This is why money is a negative energy frequency. Money leads to greed as we have just discussed.

How much money is enough money when that is all someone is focusing on? We already discussed what that answer is. It is never enough. There is no fulfillment other than having the need to constantly compete with others to have the most. It is used as a game to see who reigns superior over others when no one is superior to anyone because you are all one. You all come from the same place. That example is both money and greed. Which then leads into power.

You have put so much power and negative energy into a piece of paper that having enough of it can give you control over other human beings. You can determine other people's fate. For example, if someone does not agree with a person of power, the powerful person can do whatever they feel to them in their mind. This is because they see themselves as above the other. They are not using their wealth to better people's lives. It is about control.

Money and power over others are what caused such negativity within religions humans have created and governments and healthcare for example. But again, with such negative energies surrounding everyone, when is enough enough? It never is. That is when war occurs. Enough is never enough. So, it must expand. Money, greed, and power.

But, now for good news. A shift is coming. The energy frequency of your planet is rising at a rapid rate because people are waking up spiritually. You are realizing that all the negative events that are happening are not resonating with you. You are beginning to manifest the things that bring you joy and fulfillment, you are becoming your own bosses by coming up with beautiful ways to serve humanity in a positive way rather than being a prisoner in a job that only brings you down energetically.

The world is shifting, and you cannot stop it because that was the plan for this planet to begin with. To raise the frequency from 2D consciousness to 3D (which it is currently), and head into a 4D world where war does not exist. Hate does not exist. Power over other human beings does not exist. Money does not exist.

What is left is a race of beings who feel only love for each other. Where everyone is working together to serve each other and trading their gifts and abilities with each other for the good of others and each other's needs. Where everyone understands that we are all one, so what happens to one person is really happening to everyone. There is love, compassion, understanding, tolerance, music, humor, dancing, and pure joy. It is a choice.

Human beings manipulated the energy on this already dense planet, and turned it into intense negative energies. It was a human creation. However, energy can be manipulated as we have discussed before. Nothing is permanent. If human beings manipulated the energy to a negative frequency, human beings can raise the frequency into a positive one. It must be done by the collective at one time.

Currently, a very small portion of the world is at that point. But do not get discouraged because you are the beginning of it all. You are the start. You are lighting the way. Shine your lights brightly. You are a beacon of hope and light in the darkness of others. You cannot push these things onto others as that is unwanted negative energy. But they will eventually see your light and understand.

Again, it seems we have bounced around a lot, but everything we have said relates to each other. We hope that it all makes sense. Know that we are always sending our unconditional love and support to you now and always. Thank you for listening."

WHISPER XIII:

The Two-Week Challenge

April 4th, 2025

"Hello, friends. Kevin was up taking medication for his surgical back pain, and since channeling us helps to ease his aching pain, we thought we would take this time to address a very sensitive and important issue. Politics on your planet, and the frequency that it carries.

Now many of you watch the news, post messages about it, fight with each other about it, gloat about it, are afraid of it, and so on. We first need to address the low frequencies that politics encompasses so that you can begin to see the damage that you are actually doing to your own personal energy frequency.

When has politics ever made anyone happy? Very rarely. Because when one is happy about one thing happening, there will always be someone or something that occurs that will change your happiness and bring you down again. It is not the word politics that is the problem, but the negative frequencies that are attached to the word. Does this make sense?

Politics causes anger, frustration, fear, fighting, intolerance, exclusion, sadness, disappointment, violence, and separation. Please read those frequencies back. We call them frequencies because each of those words carry an energy frequency as everything is energy. This is extremely important to understand. With understanding you can create a change within yourself. You cannot create change without understanding.

There are many who are addicted to the news and share it with others trying to rally people against each other or prove that they are the 'right ones' when none of that is correct. It is also an interesting thing for us to see when people who claim to be very spiritual are ones who continue to post messages that cause anger and fear or intolerance of others. These 'spiritual' people say that they are living a very spiritual life.

However, one cannot live a fully spiritual life when they are living in such low frequencies. When you are living in those lower frequencies as mentioned above, the further away from Source energy, and therefore, the further away from spirituality.

Remember, the spirit realm is of the highest positive frequencies only. There are no negative frequencies. So, the lower someone's frequency, the further away they are from Source energy. So, people pretend that they are spiritual by simply saying it, but they do not practice it.

There are probably some reading this who will be very defensive at this moment because they know that this is true, they just do not want to admit this to themselves. They are living in their own false reality.

Spirituality is a state of mind. It is wakening up. It is remembering who you truly are. Which is a beautiful, positive being. So, when you are posting negativity on your social media accounts to try to rally others with anger or try to put fear in others, or those who enjoy gloating so others will get angry, you are a part of lowering the frequency of your already dense and low frequency 3D planet.

But this can change now. The idea is to shift into positive frequencies. Love, compassion, tolerance, understanding, empathy, inclusion, etc. To come together as one because we all are one. The hurt that you cause to others is causing hurt to yourself. We have discussed what spreading negative energy does to the planet, but we also have to discuss what negative energy does to yourself.

While you are posting your messages spreading fear, anger, frustration, stress and anxiety, intolerance, and gloating, you are lowering your own energy frequency to an extremely harmful level. You will notice how it will begin to affect your life around you. Negative things will begin occurring.

First, it will start out as small things, and as your negative cloud thickens, the negativity around you will become stronger where more serious issues will start to arise in your personal life. This is due to the Law of Attraction. The energy you put out will come back to you. Your thoughts, the words you say, and your actions have energies attached to them. And each energy you give off will return to you. Not out of punishment or judgement, but because you are asking the universe to give you that experience.

In other words, you are manifesting the experience or asking for it without even knowing it. We can feel some of you getting defensive again, but there is no need. It is important for you to understand this so that you can change your mindset. Being in a negative frequency is giving your power away to others, while positive frequencies are taking your power back. It is time to take your power back.

We would like to present to you a two-week challenge. This two-week challenge is about staying away from all negative energy when you are able to help it. Situations you have control over. This means no more posting messages of fear and anger to affect others because it also affects you. This means looking at life with a glass is half full mentality rather than the glass is half empty. This means choosing to surround yourself with positive energy rather than negative.

Watch only programs that make you laugh out loud and bring you joy. Listening to upbeat music that makes you want to dance as often as possible. Make a list of everything that brings you joy and go and do them. Surround yourself with people that make you smile. Dedicate some time to helping those who are in need in some way. Begin meditating to raise your frequency to a higher level and connect with your higher self and your guides. Post messages about love and kindness and compassion only if you feel the need to post something. Walk in nature when you can because earth's energy is healing.

Instead of looking at what is wrong with the world, look at what is right. Every morning say, out loud, everything that you are grateful for no matter what it is. Gratitude is so important because it raises your frequency.

A powerful thing to understand is that changing the world begins within. Be the change you want to see in the world. People will see the light you are shining and they will slowly begin to change themselves. But you need to do it for your own wellbeing energetically. Not to gloat. Not to seem more superior because no one is superior to anyone else. But for yourself. The world is nothing but mirrors. It will reflect what you are feeling within.

We hope that you will accept this two-week challenge of positivity for yourself. Because after two weeks, you will begin to feel lighter, happier, less anxious and paranoid. You will feel a noticeable change.

Please understand, two weeks is not a long time; change happens slowly. But you will notice some positive changes around you, and hopefully that will be the beginning of a new chapter for you so that you may continue on that positive journey. Trust the process.

We love you so much, and we only have your best interest at heart, as you say. But we always must say what you need to hear, not what you want to hear. Sending you love and light as always. Thank you for listening."

WHISPER XIV:

Channeling

April 6th, 2025

"Hello, our dear friends, we are back to talk with you about a topic some of you have been thinking about lately. Channeling. You may be thinking, 'what in the world am I reading?' Let us explain what channeling is first so that everyone understands.

Channeling is changing your frequency to be able to connect with us, hear us, and be able to take the information you hear and either say the information out loud or write them down. Some channel spirit guides, some other spirits, some their higher self, some other beings from other places and dimensions, and some entire collectives of beings as Kevin is currently channeling. We will introduce ourselves when it is time.

Channeling may sound like a very special ability. It is not as special as you may think. We will be using Kevin as an example since he is channeling us at the moment.

We are going to start from the beginning, talk about Kevin's life to a degree, and then we will get into channeling itself, and how you can begin to channel us right away.

Kevin did not always channel us knowingly. In fact, according to Kevin, he has only begun to hear us since last year in 2024 when his spiritual awakening began. Before that he had been in a very low frequency due to circumstances in his life. And with this low frequency, he would never have been able to hear us as clearly or even know that we existed.

However, we will say that when he was writing plays, that, too, is a type of channeling. We considered it to be a type of therapeutic exercise where he was able to get all of his emotions and frustrations out on paper. However, we are speaking of channeling in the way of hearing our messages and recording them for the purpose of this particular message you are currently reading. We digress.

He lost everything in 2022. And between 2022 to 2023, he had to rebuild his life. He knew he had to make a choice to keep going lower and lower in frequency or change it. That is when he made the decision to change everything. He made a pact with himself that from that moment forward, everything around him, including the lessons he had learned in his past would be positive experiences and lessons.

This sounds like a biography, but this is all very important to this message about channeling. We continue onward.

Since rebuilding his life and changing his frequency to a positive one, just by making the choice, he began to feel the changes. His frequency continued to soar higher and higher until we were able to connect. That is when we knew that he would be able to start hearing us loudly again (because he had heard us earlier in his life and did not know it).

From that point, things began to ramp up frequency wise. We began putting thoughts in his mind about spirituality that he had never thought of or wondered about before. He was never a religious or spiritual person before. In fact, he never took any of that seriously.

Then, we got him into reading tarot and oracle cards. We needed him to prove to himself that he was capable of reaching us for answers and guidance not only for himself but for others. Tarot is a beautiful communication tool that we highly suggest for those who wish to use it. There can be mischievous energies that can interfere with readings if you are not clear who you want to speak to, but they cannot do you harm.

Be very clear who you want to connect with. But we digress yet again. After reading tarot, we knew that he was ready to channel. He was 'tuned in' as you might say. We placed a video in front of him on his phone explaining how to channel, and gave him the desire to watch it. Once he understood the basics, he was ready.

Why are we giving you Kevin's history? Because he is no different than anyone else who is or has gone through very difficult and challenging times. He is no different than anyone who has needed guidance. He is no different than anyone else who has been at their lowest point and lowest frequencies. The situations may be different, but the frequencies are similar.

You need to understand that Kevin is not a 'chosen one' who is able to channel us. He is not 'special' in the sense that he is a part of a select group who have these capabilities. He also understands that we are not being insulting when we say that because we could never be insulting to him or anyone else. Everyone has the capabilities that Kevin does. The only thing different is that he has made the conscious choice to connect and share our thoughts and messages.

That being said, we will explain to you how Kevin connects with us, but his way of doing this is not the only way. It is one way. You must do what is right and feels good to you. First, he meditates. He has been meditating for months now, and he has been working his way to raising his frequency more and more. He meditates with the intention to connect with us.

He says it out loud before he begins: 'My intention is to connect with my spirit guides, and only my spirit guides, who are of the highest frequency and of my highest good.' He then goes into meditation. The more you meditate, the faster it will be to tune into us. It is much faster now for him to reach us than it was before. Before, he would meditate and hear nothing because he was not close enough to our frequency.

As high frequency beings, we are incapable of lowering our frequencies to an earthly level. It is just not possible. We need you to bring your positive frequency upward as high as you possibly can so that we can lower our frequency as low as we possibly can so that we can connect on the same level and be able to communicate.

Now, true, we are able to put thoughts and ideas in your mind telepathically on a regular basis because we are always guiding you, but we cannot converse with each other fully until our frequencies are aligned. We hope that this makes sense.

Back to meditation. As Kevin is meditating, he imagines himself getting into an elevator, and he says out loud 'shifting consciousness.' He is making it known that he is making this shift. He then imagines the elevator going up and up, passed his crown chakra. He imagines the elevator going as high above his physical head that he can. He imagines the door to the elevator opening and he steps out.

At this moment, he sits and waits for us to join him which is instantaneous. Then we connect. He poses a question to us or we pose a writing prompt to him. And then Kevin begins to write whatever he hears from us; trusting that whatever he is hearing is us and trusting whatever he is hearing is true.

Not everyone writes in long form like this when they automatic write or channel. Sometimes you will get one word. Sometimes a sentence we find important. It really depends on the person. Kevin is a writer by nature, so we use his writing abilities while he channels. We hope that

makes sense. It is important not to get frustrated or have expectations while you channel. If you do not hear us at all at first, it simply means a frequency adjustment needs to be made, and you will eventually have success. Practice. Practice. Practice. Trust that we are always here and we are wanting to connect with you in these ways.

Once you get the information you have received, imagine yourself getting back into the elevator and head back down to your natural frequency. Get out of the elevator and then you may open your eyes whenever you would like. If you were to open your eyes when you are of the highest frequency and not come down first, you may feel disoriented or things may feel blurred. Symptoms will subside rather quickly.

We hope that this makes sense to you. Anyone and everyone can channel us. It is your birthright to do so. You simply can choose if you want to or not. Either way we respect your decision and love you unconditionally. We are only here to help you. Trust the process.

We hope that you have enjoyed this message from us today. And we know it will reach whomever needs to read it at the precise time they need to see it. We love you, friends! Sending you love and light as always. And thank you for listening."

WHISPER XV:

Your Life Path

April 7th, 2025

"Friends, hello again from our beautiful realm, where it is always positive and always supportive. We are here to support you in every way we can, even when you feel what we are trying to do for you is not in your best interest – at the time.

Correct. Today we are talking about your life path. This is something that so many struggle with. At first, you think you are supposed to do one thing, and suddenly it switches to another, and then another. And before you know it, you are more confused than ever, and you begin to feel stuck. There is a reason for this, but to help you understand, we have permission from Kevin's higher self to help you to understand. We feel it is best to lead with examples that are real and happening at this moment in your seemingly linear world.

Kevin began with a love of theatre. In fact, that was his life for a majority of his time here on Earth. Since he was a child, he had begun to get an interest in it. His mother had nudged him to audition for a school play. She was being guided by us to nudge him in this direction. He needed to begin at this early age so that he could start on his life path. He needed confidence. Once he was performing for many years, still at a young age, he began writing scripts.

He needed to begin learning the art of creative writing; also important for his life path. After twenty years, Kevin switched to directing where he had directed over fifty productions until he turned forty-one years of age. But he stopped.

Why did he stop? This was meant to be his life path that he had begun at such an early age. This was what he was meant to do. Not necessarily. Not all is as it may seem.

Exactly a year later after his last theatre experience, he had begun hearing us again, and began his spiritual journey that he is currently on. Why does any of this matter? Because he was never off his life path. He had never strayed, never switched his soul's intended path, never was actually lost at all no matter how much he felt he was.

Let us explain why this is. He needed to grow in his talents as a leader and a writer. He needed to learn all of the skills he learned while working in theatre. These skills and lessons he learned prepped him to continue on his life path of becoming a spiritual guide. He was never off of his life path for one moment.

Without those experiences, he would never have been prepared for what is happening now and what is to come. He never would have gained his confidence to be open with others about his ideas. He never would have trusted his abilities as a writer and a leader. He never would have learned these important lessons and tools.

Now we have him writing books with us (this book you are reading being the second book, and *Divine Lessons from Your Guides* being the first), which he never would have considered if he was not already a writer.

We have him sharing these messages; he has the confidence to share his experiences openly with others without worrying about what people think of him. He has been teaching others about what he has learned spiritually and has helped guide other people through difficult times.

Because Kevin has had many moments of distress in regard to relationships, health, and career, he is now able to have the understanding necessary to truly guide and help others who may be going through similar situations, and who may feel alone. Having been through it himself, he can now be the light and support that others need.

Kevin's story is important for you to understand because you may think you are lost, but you are exactly where you are meant to be at this exact moment. There are no coincidences. In a soul contract, that we have mentioned before in a past message, you already know the lessons you will learn, the major experiences you will have, and your life path. Each moment in time is leading you into the direction you have chosen before you incarnated.

So, what do you do when you feel lost? You thought your life was going one way and suddenly there was a major shift leaving you feeling stranded. But you are not stranded. Ever.

Just like we have shown you with Kevin's life as an example, you need to start at the very beginning of your life and work your way forward. Write down or journal this if that is helpful for you to see it in writing.

Look at the significant moments in your life. Your successes, your losses, your sicknesses, your relationships, your dreams and desires in the past, the hardships. Every moment in time is a lesson and a steppingstone on your life path.

Again, you are already on your life path from the moment you were incarnated. Where are your experiences and lessons leading you? What talents and skills and tools have you acquired on your journey thus far? Why didn't certain things work out in your life when others did? How did those events lead you to where you are now? Why?

You will see how in order to have gotten where you are right now, everything that has occurred in your life had to happen at that precise moment. You were and are being led.

So, you see, life may take twists and unexpected turns, but they are not for nothing. They are each a steppingstone on your path. You may not understand it now in your present, but you will understand eventually.

As Kevin is writing this message from us, he is also realizing this to be true even more now than before.

So, if you feel lost, try the exercise of journaling your life and writing out the lessons, difficult moments, skills, and talents that you acquired up to this very moment. What patterns are you noticing? What realizations are you having? What questions suddenly have answers? This will give you not only an understanding of where you have been, but also where you are going.

You did not go through something in your life for no reason. Everything has a reason and purpose. Ask yourself why. Be inquisitive and discover. Explore. Life may seem ever mysterious, but you will see that it is not as mysterious as you may think.

We hope that this message has helped you in some way, and we are excited to continue to watch you as you continue to lay the groundwork for your beautiful path brick by brick, stone by stone. You are all warriors to take on this beautiful life challenge, and we look forward to helping you along the way. Sending you all love and light. Thank you for listening."

WHISPER XVI:

Antidepressants & Alcohol

April 8th, 2025

"Hello, friends. We are here to answer a question that was brought up about antidepressants, and if that stops you from raising your frequency. This is a great question that I am sure others would also like the answer to as well. We will address this first before moving onto the second question asked about drinking alcohol before meditation.

Let us first address depression. Depression itself is a human, physical body issue that occurs in the brain. This is of no fault of anyone that has to deal with such a thing. However, even though depression is not anyone's fault, it does have a low frequency attached to it. The idea is that you would either need to raise your frequency on your own without assistance or assistance from an antidepressant.

The purpose of an antidepressant is to raise your frequency by a controlled force so that you would no longer be in that state of depression. The effect then is that your frequency raises artificially. However, the universe does not recognize whether or not you are on a medication, rather it recognizes the fact that your frequency has raised. If someone with this illness is able to raise their frequency naturally without medication, we would always recommend trying that first, but there are degrees of depression that can make doing it on your own a challenge.

So, do antidepressants stop you from raising your frequency? No. The depression itself is what lowers your frequency. We hope that makes sense.

Let us address the second question. While antidepressants aid in raising your frequency, alcohol is a low frequency naturally. Anything that clouds judgement lowers frequency. It is a depressant and poisons the body. Again, with the word depress, it subdues, it clouds, it lowers your frequency. While in a lower frequencied state, you will notice that meditation is much more difficult. It really depends on what you are meditating for that will determine the effectiveness. If you are meditating to go to sleep, alcohol will still agitate the process, because you are still not able to focus clearly.

Now, if you are trying to meditate to connect to the higher realms, this would not be possible. In order for us to reach earthly frequencies, we can only drop our frequency so far before we can go no further. So, reaching and connecting with us is only possible while you are in your highest frequencied state. Does this make sense? So, if alcohol lowers frequency, the more trouble and difficulty you will have trying to connect with us or other high frequency energies.

It really depends on what your purpose for meditating is. We would highly recommend people to stop drinking alcohol entirely so that you are always able to connect, but mostly because it poisons the body.

While drinking alcohol, even though we will always connect telepathically, you will have a problem understanding the messages and guidance due to the cloudiness of the mind. Your mind has been slowed down and depressed. So, we always recommend not drinking alcohol. But we also understand that some enjoy it socially. It is about responsibility. That is our response to those two questions.

We thank you so much for asking us these questions and we hope we have provided you with answers that were helpful. We love you unconditionally and are always here when you need us. Thank you for listening."

WHISPER XVII:

Empathic Protection

April 9th, 2025

"Hello, dear friends, we are here to answer an important question that was brought up. You want to know about how you can protect yourself as an Empath. This is a very common question that we are delighted to answer for you, though it may have a response that you may be shocked to hear.

As an Empath, you are drawn to others' energies. You can feel when someone else is in positive or negative frequency. Kevin often calls the negative energy attached to people as 'sludge,' and since we think that is a nice visual, we will call it that as well. Empaths are drawn to the human experience of expression. They are drawn to emotions and how others emote. The issue comes into play when you are surrounded by constant or consistent chaos.

First, we must examine the chaos before we can address the Empath. The constant chaos is created when one or more human beings in the physical sense are creating negative energy, spreading it around like fertilizer to seedlings. Negative energy is very easily spread just as equally as the spreading of positive energy. Does this make sense to you?

We often give negative and positive energy on your planet the same weight. Both energies are neither good or bad necessarily; they simply give you a different experience at any given time. Now, before you came here to incarnate on your soul's mission, you decided exactly what would occur in your life. Certainly, there is some free will to maneuver about, but you will always be brought back to your path as we guide you along. During the creation of your soul contract, you decide what experiences your soul wants to have.

Again, we would like you to remember that your soul does not mind whether it is having a positive or negative experience. It simply wants experience. Your higher self holds them both at equal weight because it can learn and grow from any and all lessons. Therefore, when creating a soul contract, your soul makes sure that it has a balance of both positive and negative experiences.

Why is this important to the question? Because the people around you are simply having the experience that they had wanted when they created their soul contract. To the human mind, it is a big struggle because you look at others going through wars, injustice, and other negative experiences that you wish would end. You see them as negative experiences because of the negative frequency that it gives off. However, your soul itself feels indifferently to either frequencies. We hope that is not confusing.

Now we can address the Empath. Empaths are beautiful because they feel the energies of others. This helps you learn from watching other's behaviors. It is much like a student sitting in on a class they are not taking. You are sitting in and watching them having the experience without having the experience yourself.

However, because you are watching it happen, you can still feel what the others are feeling because you are placing yourself amongst the ones who have signed up for this experience. If you notice, when you turn off the news and stop watching it for a while, you will notice your frequency raising because you are no longer living other people's experience, only your own.

Do not misunderstand us, Empaths have a gift. This is a beautiful gift. It is the gift of understanding. You can see that things are not correct in the world, but because nothing can be done about it and there is no 'easy fix' you internalize it. This is the issue. The internalization. However, that is what an Empath is as we have stated. An internalizer. So, what do you do?

You can do two things. The first is you can separate yourself from the negative energies around you. You cannot stop someone else's experience from happening. Perhaps, only get involved when it is dealing with people in your soul group (the people closest to you in your life). Then at that point, it would involve you in their experience making it your experience at that time. Does that make sense? That is the first option.

The second option would be if you wanted to help others outside of your soul group, you must, must, must protect yourself from other people's energies. How do you do that? Remember how powerful you are as a being. You are highly connected all the time to the spirit realm. This is a dimension where everything is possible. You have those abilities which is why we often talk about manifesting and the power that human beings have.

You are called human 'beings' for a reason. The 'beings' part of it is very important because it shows you are no different from all beings in the universe and dimensionally. This is important because if you want to help other people going through difficult times and you insert yourself into the negativity, you must protect your energy by manifesting positive energy and protection.

When you do this, close your eyes, really imagine, really imagine this as you say this out loud: 'I am now protecting myself with a bubble mirror of white light and of positive energy. Only positive energy is allowed in my white light bubble of positive energy. All negative energy bounces off of my white light bubble of protection and goes back into the universe or dimension or person from whence it came. This will last all day.'

It is important to say this and truly imagine and believe what you are creating around you. This will give you protection that you need. However, if the negative energy is incredibly strong, you will need to manifest your protection more than once. We suggest protecting yourself on a daily basis in the morning when you rise and at night before you go to sleep. You can never have too much protection.

Remember, the reason you need to protect yourself is because you are choosing to put yourself in someone else's experience, and you will feel that negative energy. We hope that this makes sense for you, and we hope that you will continue to spread positivity and joy to others.

Remember to always surround yourself with positive energy which would help you as well. Self-care such as daily meditation and doing things that make you happy will also raise your frequency. Surround yourself with people that bring you joy rather than conflict.

Create boundaries with those people who have that 'sludge' attached to them. Thank you for your beautiful question, and we are sending you so much love and light. Thank you for listening."

WHISPER XVIII:

Collective Mistakes

April 13th, 2025

"Hello, friends, we are back to discuss a topic that was just discussed in Kevin's household. The question of why is it that human beings are allowed to make such large mistakes as a collective. Why is it allowed to happen?

It may seem cruel that you feel you are being forced to go through such negative experiences as a group. But please remember that your souls are trying to have various negative and positive experiences in one particular lifetime.

However, remember how we have stated before that you are all connected and that you are all one? We have given you the image of a sweater before and each of you are threads of the sweater. Each of us individually creates the whole (Source, creator of all that is). The reason that is important to understand is because each of us are having individual experiences but are connected as one having a collective experience at the same time.

This may sound confusing because it is both. The experiences that you are having individually is contributing to the group as a whole, while you are also the 'whole' simultaneously.

Now consider the 'whole' or the collective as one individual. Just as a soul must experience lessons and growth on an individual level, so must the collective on a 'whole' level. As a collective you are creating experiences to learn and grow as well. That means that as a collective, you are able to make mistakes and learn from them and therefore gain incredible and valuable knowledge.

The other important aspect of the 'whole' is that not only do you have individual soul contracts, but there are also collective contracts. This is why you are all considered warriors. You have decided to come to earth at this particular point in time to complete a particular mission as a collective, together, all at once, while also having your own individual experiences. You have decided as a collective that it is now time to begin raising the frequency of this planet from 3D to 4D consciousness.

You have learned so many lessons as a collective of souls that you no longer wish to keep this planet the same. You are growing tiresome because war and injustice is no longer serving you. Did it ever serve you? It served you once before because there were important lessons that had to be learned as a collective.

However, once a lesson is learned and you feel that you have grown from the experience, why would you want to take that class over again for no reason? You do not. So, a change or shift must be made in collective consciousness. Does this make sense?

So, if you consider the collective as one being on this planet, imagine the collective as a child. The child needs to learn in order to grow and understand and develop. Learning difficult lessons helps the child understand what they should and should not do.

For example, if a child sees a flame. It may look beautiful, so they feel the need to want to touch the flame. No matter how much a parent or guardian tells that child not to touch the flame because it is hot and will hurt them, the child becomes obsessed with needing to know what it is like for themselves. So, as a child, they finally touch the flame and they burn themselves. The likelihood of them wanting to touch a flame or fire in general again will be decreased highly.

The same is true as a collective. You are learning and growing as human beings. You are realizing what does and does not work as a team and what does and does not serve you. This is why there is so much division on your planet at the moment. You are all trying to figure out what is correct and what is not. What is right, what is wrong? Who is right, who is wrong? Where is right, where is wrong? How is right, how is wrong?

It seems like an impossible jigsaw puzzle with a million pieces that have been thrown everywhere out of the box. But in order for the frequency of the planet to raise, all must be on the same wavelength. All must be on the same frequency. Only then can this planet truly become a 4D conscious planet. The billion piece jigsaw puzzle must be completed.

This is no easy task, as you can already see occurring in your world, and can be extremely painful and frustrating. This is why there is so much anger and frustration and injustice in your world. The collective is making decisions blindly hoping they are making the right choices. You are currently putting your collective finger to the flame. And this is painful. This is why you are all warriors. You are an important part of this process. You understand the assignment. You wish to not repeat this course. You understand that there are better ways, peaceful ways.

Eventually, everyone will see that and the massive shift will occur. Until then, you are learning and growing together. You are doing what others have shied away from because it is an uncomfortable feeling to be on your planet at this time. But know you are doing so much good as you, yourself, are a massive part of this new shift.

We hope that this message makes sense to you and we also hope it has reached you at the appropriate time. As always, jigsaw puzzle experts, we are sending you love and light. Thank you so much for listening."

WHISPER XIX:

Eating Meat

April 27th, 2025

"Hello, beautiful souls, we received a question asking us: is it wrong to eat meat? First, you must understand that everything you do is a choice. Are you questioning whether you should eat meat because you do not want to see other animals die? Are you questioning it because you are seeing others doing it, and therefore are questioning whether you should eat meat or not?

If you do not feel that it is right to eat other animals, then you should not do it because it is against what you believe. However, if you are not eating meat because others are telling you to stop, that is a different story. For something to matter, it must matter to you. If you were the only person alive, and there was an abundance of animals around you, and you had no one around you to influence your decision, would you eat them?

It is important to go to this extreme because what matters is what you feel about it inside. When the collective raises their frequency to 4D consciousness in your planet's future, you will all realize that killing things for food will no longer serve you as it does not serve them either. A life is a life is a life. But in order for that to happen, the entire collective must awaken so that there is a unanimous understanding of this concept.

Human beings will discover other means of nutrition. Since the collective is only at the beginning of the awakening, this concept does not fully exist. In fact, there will even be a point where human beings will no longer require food or water at all. But that is not a reality in this moment as you keep ascending from 3D to 4D to 5D consciousness.

During the full awakening of your planet, you will be coming up with new ideas on how to receive the proper nutrition for your bodies without harming other living things. The nutrients are currently the issue. Because your physical body requires certain nutrients to survive, the decision to not eat other living things becomes a challenge. Some have figured it out, and others find it daunting. The choice is yours and always will be yours.

At this point in the awakening, you have choices. Are you the one killing the animals for the food? If so, and you find killing other living things wrong, then do not kill them anymore. If the animal has sacrificed itself already and you buy the meat from a grocery store, you had no part in its death and can live with a clear conscience. Not eating the meat that is already there does not change the fact that that living animal has already passed. If you find the sight of meat repulsive, and every time you look at it, you can feel the animal's death, then perhaps eating meat is not for you.

This is a choice based on how you, as a human being, feel about eating meat. If you observe other animals in the animal kingdom, they also must survive. It is true that these animals are 2D consciousness beings, or instinct-centered consciousness, but all beings have souls. And if all souls are making decisions prior to their incarnation, then they already know what they are expecting of themselves from themselves. Does this make sense? They understand the assignment when they come to Earth, just as you understand your own assignment as you continue to incarnate.

The lesson here is to think for yourself. What feels right for you? What feels correct to you? If you did not have any influence from others, would your answer change or shift? If you decide that not eating other living things is wrong, how far do you take it? Do fish count? Do plants count? Trees and plants and vegetation have life too. There are even those who can feel the spirit from such plant life.

So, do you no longer eat plants and vegetation? How far are you willing to take it? What makes one life, whether animal or plant life, easier to kill than another? Both are equally important to the Earth.

Remember that your physical bodies currently need nutrients from such living things around you. Without it, you cannot survive. If you look to everything that lives in the world, it feeds off of something to survive. Everything needs nutrients to continue living and surviving. Everything.

So, with all of that in mind, what is your own decision that you have made for yourself? What feels best for you? Someone who does not eat meat is not better than someone who does. Even a vegetarian must eat plant life to survive, and those plants were living at one time. You buy a bouquet of flowers from a store. Those flowers will die, but you still bought them. Does this make sense?

Do what is right for you and what makes you happy and fulfilled without feeling you are a terrible person or feeling like your frequency is lowering. However, it does matter what types of foods you put in your body. Lots of sugar and processed foods and chemicals will lower frequency. We suggest what you call 'organic' and 'clean eating.' That is best for your nutrition for your physical bodies.

We hope that this answer has helped you, and we hope that you continue to raise your frequency and find your bliss. We send you so much love and light as always, and thank you for listening.

WHISPER XX:

The Fear in Religion

September 23rd, 2025

"Hello, dear friends. It has been some time since we have spoken to you. We are here to talk to you about your religions of the world. It seems as though religion continues to be an issue of so much separation and so much negativity. You think that if you do not believe a certain way, that you will be damned for all eternity to some horrific place of punishment. This is far from truth.

We do not believe in using tactics that utilize fear as a tool to get a certain result. This is not how we feel or behave, yet, as the same fractals of Source that human beings are, many believe that causing fear in others is necessary to keep control. Many times, religion is used as a weapon to cause anger and fear amongst you, keeping the frequency of the collective down to low levels. This low frequency prevents you from connecting to higher frequencied energies.

Why is that important to you? Because with a low vibrational frequency, one is able to be manipulated and controlled. As beings with free will, it silently removes your free will in the guise of a higher power practice. Your free will is your own to do with as you please. It is all about choice.

What is happening on the Earth currently? You are witnessing the beginning of a massive change, a massive shift in your world. You are seeing what you will and will not accept in your societal systems.

These systems will eventually dissolve almost completely. Time does not exist, but in your perceived linear time frame, that could be anywhere from a few hundred years to more depending on the free will of the collective and how much each individual chooses to fight the shift. And there will be a fight to stop this shift as it relinquishes control.

Whose religion reigns supreme? None. Religion is a human creation. You can believe whatever you want to believe whenever you want to believe it. It does not matter. You can choose to believe in everything or nothing at all. It does not matter. You are loved regardless. There is no punishment for believing a certain way, and there is no punishment for not believing a certain way. You can believe the Seven Dwarfs from Snow White are your gods and that is fine, you are loved unconditionally. We love humor.

Look at the ascended masters from your species: Jesus, Buddha, Babaji, Quan Yin, etc. There are many, many ascended masters. Who is better? No one. It does not matter who is better because there is no better. There is only their teachings of love and kindness that matters. Ascending only means you do not have to return to Earth to learn lessons. They have already learned them and have not had to return unless they so choose.

Just as they have ascended, you are also ascending. This is the whole point of you choosing to be here lifetime after lifetime, trying to learn and grow as much as possible so that you do not need to return again. Does your life as a soul stop then? No. They can choose to live in higher plains of existence where their energies are most needed. You will also eventually get to that same decision of: what's next for me in this eternity?

We now circle back to religion. We see people using religion as a weapon against others. Excluding people who are different than you, telling people if they do not follow your every word they will be damned. They cannot be damned because there is no fire burning place of eternal punishment. That, too, is a man-made creation to keep you under certain people's control. This creates a lot of fear about the transition process, or what you perceive as death. They think they will go to a nightmarish place where they are burned for all of eternity.

Side note: as energy, and as creators, you are able to create the experience you wish after you transition. This means that if you believe you will go to a nightmarish place when you leave here, that is the experience you will create for yourself until you decide you want it to change and you have had enough of it. This is why there is much power in suggestion.

Telling people they are going to burn in Hell for something actually does affect the person energetically. It places fear deep within them causing them to have that experience. But again, all you must do is say you have had enough of that nightmarish experience, and you will be out of it as quick as the thought itself.

Who can talk to Source (God)? Everyone. We are all fractals of it. For someone to tell you that you must go through them to speak to it is absolutely not true. Source lives inside of you. Speak to it. Listen for its response. Feel its love wrapped inside of you like a hug. Source lives within and always has been.

What is religion good for? It is good because it gets people to connect with Source and Source energy. It is good because it raises frequency for those who speak to us daily in what you call prayer. Prayer is simply a type of meditation and manifestation. But the name with which you call it does not matter. The names do not matter.

Another example of naming is you call certain groups of beings angels, but that is a human created term. We do not call ourselves angels but more like messengers. But again, the name does not matter. What matters is the purpose with which you are speaking to us. We can only assist if you ask us to according to the Law of No Interference.

Religion is also good for community. Some of you need to feel like you are a part of something greater than yourself, which you already are, but the energy of a group combined becomes stronger which keeps you returning; unless you are returning so that you are not punished, then we suggest not going.

The reason you are doing something is everything. It is all about intention. With good reason comes positive frequency, with negative reason comes negative energy. So, even if you are attending a religious service, which has its positive energy attached, but you are attending because if you do not go you will be damned for eternity, is attaching a negative energy to it. Does this make sense?

We do ask that when you attend a service of any religious business organization, to listen to the positive and beautiful messages, and filter out the negative messages built in to keep you in fear and in line. It is important to think for yourself, not having others think for you.

Make your own decisions and your own path. Create the energy around yourself that you wish to envelop yourself in. Do what you feel is best with the highest intention of love and gratitude. Do whatever it is that makes you feel you are serving others best.

Following those guidelines will make you so much happier and more fulfilled in your life. It is all about raising your frequency as high as possible. As always, we send you love and light. Thank you for listening."

WHISPER XXI:

Reflection

October 2ⁿᵈ, 2025

"Hello dear friends. We have come to discuss the topic of reflection. Reflecting on one's life is so important because it teaches you lessons throughout your lives. Why did you behave that way? Why did you make that decision? What occurred in your life after you made those certain decisions?

We ask you to take moments to either write things out in the process of journaling or record yourself speaking aloud for your own archival knowledge. While going through moments in your life and really trying to figure out the root cause, you can then begin the healing process. Without reflection you cannot learn and without learning you cannot grow and if you cannot grow you must take the class again until you begin to learn.

Nothing is coincidental. There is divine purpose for everything that occurs. This is where reflection is important. What made you lash out at that person? Why did you get so angry? Why do you doubt yourself? What occurred to put that thought into your head?

You see, there is always a reason for everything that occurs. What were you meant to learn, dear one? Why did you have to go through such trauma in your life? Why was that necessary? If you look at the incident and not see what came from it, it makes the incident purposeless. But nothing is purposeless. How did that very event or events shape you into who you are today? How did those events teach you in your life?

Perhaps you were mistreated as a child and now you are a social worker helping other children. Perhaps you went through abusive relationships and you now assist those going through similar situations. You see? It was not for not. It was for your divine purpose. Your life path. We do not wish you to be in pain or go through such difficult moments, but where would you be without those moments? Where would your life have gone? In what direction would you have been led?

You have a certain purpose in your life, and not going through anything at all would lead you to wander aimlessly without any direction. The past events in your lives shapes your presents. It may be unpleasant at the time, but through healing you can see the purpose. This is where reflection assists you. It is the realizations that guide you even when you think you are not being guided.

Through reflection you can heal yourself. Reflection is healing. Reflection is healing. It is healing. Reflection has that power, and you have that power within you. It is time to write down or record your reflections. When you reflect, the positive lessons emerge. What once was hidden comes to light. Write down what positive lessons were learned from the experiences? How can you use what you learned to help others in the world heal?

We ask you to consider doing this exercise so that you can have a better understanding of yourself and your purpose. Life is lessons and growth. If your response is there are no lessons in what had occurred, you have more reflecting and more work to do. Trust that you are always where you are meant to be. Trust the process. Trust that there is a higher purpose for everything.

Also give yourself love, compassion, and grace. Do not judge yourself because you are not your past, you are only your present. We love you very much, dear ones. And as always, we thank you for listening."

WHISPER XXII:

The Human Connection

October 10th, 2025

"Hello, dear ones. We see you, we hear you, we love you. Let us talk about connections. Connections between you and the human beings around you. Connection is everything, and we will tell you why.

Many human beings are focused on the wrong things. Materialism. What you have in your possession: whether that is money, houses, cars, and other things that you continually fill your life with. But you have heard this saying before and we will say it again: 'You cannot take it with you.' You cannot bring your homes or cars or money with you. Why?

Because that is not what your experience is about. It is not about where you work, how much money you make, how many things you possess. It is about the genuine connections you make during this current experience. The love you show to others. The joy you bring. That is what matters.

If we were to take away all your possessions right now, what would you have left? What emotional connections would be left over? If you are a highly materialistic person, and do not surround yourself with loving connections or you have treated people badly in your past, if we were to take all your possessions away from you, what would you be left with?

If your answer is that your life would still be full of positive connections around you, that is a beautiful thing. If you say you would be isolated with no human connections, then how can you change that today?

As human beings, you are not meant to be isolated and alone. You are there to connect, and through connections you share your light with the world. Your light is healing. It brings joy and happiness within it. That is why it must be shared. Does this make sense?

If you enjoy isolating yourself from people, what type of healing is necessary to move forward so that you are not so isolated? There are reasons for everything: root causes. What is the root cause of your isolation? That shadow part of yourself must be healed. There is pain there that needs to be addressed.

We wish for you to be happy and fulfilled at a soul level, and that does not include your material possessions. That means healthy, beautiful relationships. Be around those who make you laugh or make you smile. Be with those who will listen to your pain and help to lift that weight off of your shoulders.

Material possessions give an immediate joy. But that joy dissipates after a short period of time. Then you find you must buy something else that excites you until that joy wears off and so on and so on. It is a cycle.

Objects to do not last for eternity, but your beautiful connections with others do.

We hope that you will take this under consideration as you continue to journey on your path. We are always here for you, and we love you very much. We are so proud of your bravery. Thank you for listening."

WHISPER XXIII:

Beauties of the World

October 13th, 2025

"Hello friends, we are here to talk to you about the beauties of the world. There is much beauty around you all the time. They are to remind you of home. Since earth is the only place where souls are meant to forget, we have placed bits and pieces of home all around you to help you through difficult moments and to remind you of where you came from.

When we say 'we' have placed everything there for you, it is because we and you are creators with the Divine. We are the Divine just as you are the Divine. Therefore, we have all created what you see around you both positively charged and negatively charged.

But this post is not about emphasizing the negative, it is about looking at the positive, so we will continue there.

As above so below. You have heard of this phrase and it has many meanings that are all true. We are focusing on the beauties you see. As we mentioned before, this planet was created as an experiment. To see how souls would react when forced to forget where they came from and they are given the task to learn the most challenging lessons there are to learn. We are observers and you are all the field workers. You are slowly but surely creating a society that resembles 'home.'

We did not say you were there yet. You have many hundreds of years to go before this will be accomplished. However, you are at the beginning stages, where you are recognizing the cracks in all the systems that control you and others. Through these cracks, you will discover what is best for everyone as a whole rather than those as individuals. Because you are not individuals. You are all one from the same place.

We digress. As we mentioned before, we have placed beautiful reminders of home everywhere you look. The Divine architecture of a tall, beautiful tree. A sunset with colors in the sky you could only imagine. Everything natural is a reminder.

Everything is alive. The air, the water, the earth, the fire. All is living. Just because it does not breathe like animals do does not mean they are not living. As souls you have no use for breathing, only your physical bodies do, but you are still very much alive.

Look around you. Every time you feel a beautiful breeze on your face, every time you see a beautiful lake, every time you drive and see the beautiful trees and flowers or leaves changing. Every time you see a sunset and sunrise –

know that those are reminders of home. To remind you that you are much greater than you even believe.

We ask that you now look at the beautiful life around you as reminders of where you truly come from. Know that you are never as far away as you feel. You are always close. And know that there is more love for you than you could ever imagine.

As above so below. You are beautiful and perfect as you are because you were created this way. We are sending you so much love as always. Please remember to talk to us, we are always listening. We are with you, and we will always respond. Take good care, sweet and brave friends. We admire your incredible courage and strength. And thank you for listening."

WHISPER XXIV:

Universal Balance

October 16ᵗʰ, 2005

"Hello, dear ones. We are here to talk about universal balance.

You are incredibly brave to be here right now. You all have very specific missions whether you are aware of it or not. Some of your missions are to admit light naturally to help raise the frequency of this planet. You are doing an amazing job of doing this, and we first wanted to say how proud we are of you.

Now we shall go into our lesson for you. Universal balance. The universe must be in balance at all times. Without balance there is collapse. You are a part of the universe, therefore you must be in balance at a soul level.

You are here to experience and educate yourself and others through experience. Without actual experience, you would only know the fundamentals of life rather than fully living it and experiencing it.

For example: you read how to change a tire in a booklet. You fully know how to change a tire based on your book knowledge on the subject. But when it is time to have hands on experience of changing a tire, you are putting your book knowledge to the test. Once you have completed changing a tire, you now have firsthand experience. This is what your soul craves.

This means that your soul wants to know everything there is to know and understand first hand. what it is like to have more masculine energy or feminine energy, what it is like to have a strong body versus a weak body, what it is like to treat people poorly versus be treated poorly.

This is education. You are in school to fully understand everything there is to know about human life. This may sound daunting to the human mind because there is only so much your mind can handle before something is no longer comprehensible.

But do not fret, we will explain. Your higher self or oversoul as some call it, is a very loving being capable of anything and everything all at once. Your soul is already a loving and beautiful being of light.

However, when a fractal of your soul is then put into the energetically dense human world, it gives your soul the rare opportunity to discover and explore emotions and feelings it normally would not encounter.

Low density emotions are attached to the human brain: fear, anger, doubt, anxiety, stress, judgment of others, and the difficulty of loving oneself. That is why earth is one of the most challenging places a soul can choose to incarnate, and a soul must be advanced enough to be a candidate. You are on earth currently, therefore, you were ready.

Back to balance. Your soul understands that when it wants to have an experience, it will need to create balance either within the same lifetime or across multiple lifetimes. But time does not exist as it does on your planet. We can bend and twist time and manipulate it so that you can learn the necessary lessons needed to move forward in your soul journey.

So, what does this mean? For example: you are cruel to another human being. You exclude them or are even physically abusive. The scale has now been tilted in one direction. Imbalance. The next lifetime, in order to create that balance, your soul will need to learn what it is like to be physically abused and treated cruelly.

Another example: you are what you call racist against certain people in one life, and the next life you must understand what it feels like to be treated the way you treated others before. Final example: you are wealthy, and you do not take that opportunity to give your wealth to others in need and you keep it to yourself. Greed. In the next life you will be poor with no assistance.

Balance must be restored. This is not out of punishment. This is education. Your soul has a desire to fully understand. Once you understand that treating people poorly does you actual harm, you will be less likely to do that in another lifetime. You are free to explore and discover as you are there, but always remember that balance must always be restored in every situation.

This also means positively as well. If you do something amazing for others in a lifetime. Perhaps you help the homeless or serve humanity in some beautiful way, you will receive that treatment in return in your next lifetime. This is not a reward, but balance. This is soul education. We also understand that it is very challenging.

You are the brave souls that agreed to do this earth experience. The more you learn and experience, the more your soul grows. This is about graduating from this school so that you no longer need to return.

So, how can you incorporate all of what we have discussed in your life today? Knowing balance must always be restored, how can you begin to change the way you treat others today? How can you bring a positive shift to humanity?

It is a ripple effect, just as one throws a stone in the water and it ripples outward in every direction. An act of kindness spreads which creates a bigger ripple and a bigger ripple. You alone are changing the world just by making positive choices for yourself and others.

Be the beautiful ripple of love. Because how you treat others will affect how you are treated soon enough. And as the Divine always says: there is no time limit to learn these lessons, you have eternity.

We hope that we have not carried on too long for you. Know that we love you dearly, and we cannot wait to see the beauties you bring to this world. Thank you for listening."

WHISPER XXV:

Negative Energy

October 23rd, 2025

"Hello, dear ones. We are here to discuss a very important topic of negative energy. Why does it exist on Earth? Why is it necessary to have negative energy within your experience as a human being?

These are questions we would like to address at this time. It is a moment for you to remove yourself from what feels like your reality and step outside of it looking inward. We are asking you to be an observer at this moment as you reflect on our message to you.

There are places in the universe that do not hold such negative energy as Earth does. We have explained before that coming to Earth is a choice by you for higher education. When you were living other lives on much higher energetic levels elsewhere, you were learning about Source and Source energy. You learned about the cosmos and the way the universe works. You understood that living beings are all one because we all share an energetic Source. You also learned how to connect to Source energy on an intuitive level.

125

Intuitive abilities were not only taught so they could grow, but they were celebrated.

Those were very important lessons to learn at that time. Those lessons were preparing you for the experiences as human beings you are now. Why did you need all the prep work? It is like sending a seven year old to a PhD program and expecting them to succeed. It is not realistic and doing so would set a soul up for failure. Since that is a negative frequency, that is not possible. You had to learn over many lifetimes to gain the knowledge necessary for you to come to this challenging university to put your past knowledge to the test.

This means that you agreed to forget everything so that you could eventually find yourself again from what you perceived as nothing. But it was not nothing. You have ancient knowledge inside of you, and you use it all the time whether or not you believe you do. That is your own specific journey and mission you are on.

We needed to explain that so that we could go back to negative energy. Why is it here? You are given a myriad of choices in these human lifetimes. You are given the opportunity to choose between positive or negative energy. Light and dark and everything in between. You are given the opportunity to choose between opposites with much gray area in between. You are given the opportunity to find what the right path is for you.

If you choose a more negative route, it is okay. You are not judged for your actions or choices. However, during your mission review, you have the opportunity to see how your choices affected others and how the ripples you created were received. With that new knowledge, you are able to come back and try it again with a different set of scenarios. Just as when you retake a test, they have different questions; you are given a new set of circumstances to try out your new found knowledge and try again.

Without negative energy, how does one learn these most challenging lessons? If your only choice is positive energy you cannot grow fully from that experience. However, you grow a lot through negative experiences. You not only grow as a human being, but at a soul level. This is the whole point of coming to this university. If you are not growing and learning, there is no reason for you to come here. Education must continue.

The more difficult situation is that you are placed on Earth with others at various levels; some just starting out, and others who are graduating soon. You must observe others. The student becomes the teacher and the teacher becomes the student. Observe. Life is a mirror. Look inward and be the change you wish to see in the world. If you, yourself, are combative, you will be surrounded by others of that same experience. Energy is magnetic and is drawn to those of the same frequency.

If you do not like what is happening externally, it is time to fix what is happening internally. It begins within you, not outside of you. So, you see, negative energy must exist to be able to learn the lessons you are learning here. Some may say that it is very unpleasant, and we understand that it is difficult, however, you have a much higher mission to spread love and joy to others so that it will spread to others and ripple outward.

Do not exclude others unless you, yourself, wish to be excluded. Do not show others anger unless you wish to be met with anger. A mirror.

This is a small piece of a study guide to help you understand negative energy, and we hope that you understand better now. We love you very much and we are rooting for your success always. You are the brave warriors.

Sending you love, and as always, thank you for listening."

WHISPER XXVI:

A Review in Life

October 27th, 2025

"Hello, dear ones! We are here today to talk about the life review again. We have mentioned this before, but we are here to help you to reflect on it in another way.

When you transition back to your home realm, after your current human experience has come to an end, you go through a life review.

This is done in various ways depending on the specific soul going through it. During the life review you will see parts of your life where you treated others well, and when you did not. You also see where you treated yourself well, and when you did not.

You relive each experience as a final exam of sorts so that you may learn fully for your next incarnation. Each experience is shown to you and you relive it, not only how you felt in the moment, but how the other person felt in the moment.

If you made someone smile by making them feel good about themselves, you feel how that felt for them. That energy pulsates through you. If you punched someone and made them feel pain, you will feel exactly what it felt like when you hit that person.

This life review is not done out of judgment or punishment, it is done to educate. Once you learn how something felt, it will be much easier to make certain choices in your next incarnations. This is important for what we want to discuss today.

Knowing you have a life review where you have the opportunity to feel the positive and negative impact you have on others' lives, how will you make changes to your life and behavior today to go in a more positive direction?

This is something that is normally taught after the life review, but we are giving you the opportunity to reflect on this now while you are still in your current human experience.

Since you now understand about the life review occurring after your transition, we ask that you form your own life review up to this point in your incarnation now. Who have you brought so much joy to? Who did you make laugh or feel better when they were down? How have you loved yourself and shown yourself that love?

The same for the negative: Who have you harmed? How can you be a more positive force moving forward? Who have you purposefully excluded due to peer pressure or religious pressure? What behaviors need to be addressed so

that you can be a more positive influence? Why did you behave that way? What needs to be addressed within you, from your past, that is the root cause of your behaviors and actions?

Creating your own life review now gives you the opportunity to be a more positive influence in the world in the present rather than waiting till your next incarnation to put what you have learned to the test. This is not to beat yourself up; it is to learn from the past so that you may move forward with more light in the present. In order to learn from yourself, you must be honest with yourself.

We hope that you will attempt this life review reflection, and we hope that it will create positive changes in your current lifetime.

We are sending you so much love, light, and gratitude, dear ones. And as always, thank you for listening."

WHISPER XXVII:

The Quest for Perfection

October 29th, 2025

"Dear ones, we are here to talk about your quest for perfection. You naturally, as humans, want everything to be perfect. Perfect life, perfect home, perfect family, etc. the reason this is, is because you come from a place of balance and harmony. Your sense memory remembers where you truly come from. Perfection is not something that is desired because everything is already and always has been in balance and order.

Now you are a human being living this human experience for a time, and things are not as perfect as you would want. This is normal to feel this way. As we said before in other messages to you, there are clues everywhere as reminders of your true existence. You come from a realm of balance put into a realm of imbalance. This is truly difficult to handle sometimes.

An example of you searching for perfection that occurred this morning: As Kevin got ready for work, he was trying so hard to keep quiet this morning so that he would not wake up his partner, Armando. He attempted to do things perfectly to make the least amount of sound possible to accomplish this.

He closed the bathroom door slowly, he bought a new electric toothbrush that was not as loud, he even held the metal piece on his belt so that he could get his pants on without the belt making loud dinging noises.

Kevin does not mind if we embarrass him a bit.

Back to Kevin's 'quiet challenge' this morning. As Kevin was trying to achieve this quiet perfection, his body unknowingly began to tense up, his hands were a little more stiff, his body was a little more tense as well. This tenseness, as he discovered, would have the exact opposite effect.

He slowly got out of bed carefully and knocked his legs into the nightstand. Then he quietly walked over to the bathroom door and shut it so carefully that while carefully releasing the lever, it made a loud noise because the door had not actually been fully closed.

While putting on his pants, he grabbed the metal piece on his belt so there was no noise, but stuck his leg through the hole of the pants where it got stuck and almost forced him to the floor. Getting back in bed to write this currently, he quietly and carefully grabbed a second pillow as a headrest almost knocking over a water glass.

Another Kevin example: he has just begun including pendulum readings for people. We had had Kevin include the pendulum after some time as another tool in his toolbox.

However, just as anyone must practice training their bodies for workouts, Kevin must continue training so that the pendulum will be a great addition to his readings. However, Kevin expected his first, full hour-long pendulum reading to be perfect with a lot of evidential results.

He was so focused on having the perfect pendulum reading, that he began to ignore the actual evidence that was occurring. The evidence was not perfect or strong enough for him or what he had expected.

However, there was evidence given during the reading. A connection gets stronger as time goes on, and as connection gets stronger, more evidence will show itself. Nothing happens immediately and nothing happens perfectly.

Kevin began to get down on himself even wondering if he should continue with the pendulum. But he must. It is like picking up forty-pound weights the first time you decide to weight lift. It is not possible. But with training, everything is possible. Strength and connection come in time.

Do not be discouraged when your best does not produce the results you are expecting right away. Keep training. But when you expect perfection, you are ignoring the progress you have achieved. Just like Kevin ignoring the evidence that came through in his first, full pendulum reading. His connection to the pendulum and board will get stronger over time. Patience is key to everything.

Why are we telling you all of this? Because when you try to reach perfection, which does not exist in your experience, that is when you make even more mistakes. The harder you try, the more your body naturally tenses up, causing the reverse effect of what you actually wanted.

In trying to be perfect he made more mistakes or had ignored certain evidence than if he had just done what he was going to do. He would have made less noise by not trying so intently not to make noise. Does this make sense?

Instead, we want you to relax your body. Remove the tension that you hold within you trying to be perfect all of the time. It is not only mental but physical as well. Tension can cause headaches and migraines, and physical aches and pains and body fatigue elsewhere in the body, and you do not deserve that in your life.

Do not strive to be perfect, but just strive to be a good person, doing the best you can with knowledge that you have gathered from past experiences. You are perfect in our eyes no matter how imperfect you feel you are. Trust. Your best must be good enough because you can do no better than your best.

Instead, strive to be happy, fulfilled, loving, compassionate, grateful, and giving. Those are what you should strive for to the best of your ability every single day.

We understand that this is a long message, but it is an important one. We hope this helped you. We are sending you so much love as always, and thank you so much for listening, dear friends."

WHISPER XXVIII:

Angels

October 30th, 2025

"Hello, dear ones. We would like to discuss a topic that is brought up on a daily basis from millions of people all over your world. Angels.

We, the collective speaking now, are a subcategory of who you call angels. We love creating names for our group because human beings have the need to name everything. So, collectively, we have called ourselves the Fire Force.

Why did we choose this name for ourselves? Fire is the fire of creation. The want to create because we are all creators. And we mentioned the force as we are also protectors. Together we are protective creators. We assist when asked to assist. But another part of our job is to restore balance when restoration is necessary.

You call us angels, but that is not what we call ourselves. That is a human term because you want to place name tags on everything. So, we accept. We consider ourselves more like messengers because we bring messages of healing and assistance and protection to those who ask for it.

However, you have placed the term angel on us, which has a vibration that we understand. Everything holds an energy frequency. Even thoughts and single words have frequencies. If you consider a dial on a radio, you know what your favorite station is to play because of the music you enjoy listening to.

The same is for those in our realms. If you are looking to connect with your grandmother who has passed, you are already adjusting your frequency naturally to connect. If you want assistance from us or other messengers, you change the dial to the frequency that connects. You do this naturally.

This is why you have placed these names on us. It gets you to our frequency faster as the term angel now holds that frequency. So, when you call upon us, we are connected with you.

Now, many of you have been misinformed and we would like to clear things up. From this point on we will call ourselves the term you have given us. Angels. Many of you think that we are above you; that we are more special and more powerful than you as souls and beings.

This is not correct. It is only a different frequency. Let us explain: think of the earth. See how there are different patches of land in the world. You call them countries or even bigger still, continents. There is no continent that is better than another, but they are all together in the same place. We are simply from a different continent. But please know that this was by choice just as you chose.

When we were all created, we had choices to make. How were we going to create together? There are contracts signed, what you would call contracts anyway. We call them understandings. It is understood. We have the ability to choose where you want to go and what you want to do. We wanted to be a messenger of love and peace and protection. And so it is.

We then formed what you would call cohorts. Groups with the same goal working as one because we are all one. Each group has a different job. We decided to help and observe, and you decided to be field workers creating beautiful worlds and raising the frequencies of each planet to match the Source energy.

Both jobs are equally important. You could not do your job without us and we could not do our job without you. Equal. We are equal not separate. We are your friends from another part of your realm.

Now let us speak of what you call Archangels. You enjoy ranking things from best to worst. That is unnecessary. Hierarchy does not exist. You put others on pedestals above you as though you are not powerful yourself. This is not the case. Let us explain.

When something happens to your car, do you take your car to your local doctor or do you take your car to a mechanic? Please do not take your car to your doctor. He will not know what to do for you. Take it to the mechanic. Once the mechanics look at the car you will have one or two that may be more experienced. Let us call them specialists. These specialists have the experience to be able to fix more complicated problems. Archangels are specialists.

But is this specialist better than your doctor? Is the specialist better than other mechanics? No. They are all important equally. Is the car specialist more important than someone who entertains another and makes them laugh? No. So, you see? You rank other beings above you when there are no pedestals. It is simply a different frequency; a different place. No better, no worse.

Kevin once asked us if we had ever incarnated before. Not all of us. There are a select few who walk amongst you now. For the rest, we are not interested. We enjoy what we do to assist you. We do consider you very brave, however. To be the ones who volunteered to have this experience is courageous and admirable. It shows how powerfully strong you are. You are in the trenches doing some of the most difficult work in your universe. We are proud of you in every step you take and every move forward. You are celebrated.

We are the Fire Force, and we are delighted to speak with you. We can always hear you, but we cannot step in for two reasons:

The first is we cannot step in if it is part of your soul's path. We are not able to interfere with the choices and contracts you had made prior to your incarnation. Second, you must be specific in what group of angels you would like assistance from. We love when you are specific.

Kevin calls on the angels of driving each time he gets into his vehicle. He calls on the angels of dentistry before going to the dentist. He calls on the angels of surgery before his surgical procedures. Like different states in one country, different states provide a different experience. So, be specific; we love that.

We hope that you have found this message interesting, but we have heard your thoughts about angels many times, and we wanted to take the time to speak to you about the subject. We love you so much, and we continue to admire your incredible bravery and strength. And as always, thank you for listening."

WHISPER XXIX:

After the Transition

October 31st, 2025

"Friends, it is us again to discuss what your experience will be after you transition back to your true home and reality; when you come home from your school of learning and experience.

This is where we get excited because it can literally be anything you wish it to be. Let us explain because we understand that that is vague, and we do not wish it to be.

Everything is energy, correct? This energy has consciousness. This consciousness that you are is a beautiful light source capable of creating. You are always creating your experience even now while in your physical forms you have chosen.

There is a law that must be in place for those who decide to have the Earth experience. The Law of Forgetfulness. This law must be in place because of the low density you have chosen to witness and feel firsthand. Since you come from a place of the highest frequency, it is too much of a shock for you to remember where you came from.

Remembering would cause people to want to end their experience on Earth much sooner than their higher-selves contractually agreed to. Though there are what you call exit points throughout your experience when a soul can decide to continue the simulation or start a new one. We will discuss exit points in another message to you.

Why is all of this important for this discussion? Because you are immersed into the Earth experience. You do not see anything than what is around you and physical. Some are taught that certain things occur after you go back, and some believe nothing occurs when you go back. Due to the Law of Forgetfulness, you are given a type of amnesia in a sense.

Earth is a wonderful place to feel what it is like to believe in all things and nothing at all and everywhere in between. It is your choice. We understand that this means people are influenced by others, but that is part of the experience you have chosen.

So, because you cannot remember where you are from, though many do over time as they awaken and remember, you are influenced by many things on Earth. Religion is one that is a heavy influencer.

Because of this, when you transition, so that things are not as jarring, you will create the experience you have seen for yourself to help you through. For example: if you are a devout Catholic, and you have believed everything told to you for your entire human life, that does not immediately go away when you transition back. The 'amnesia' wears off slowly. Therefore, you may create a vision of a very biblical scene. Many see the Tree of Life or a beautiful garden, etc. You create what you think you will see in that moment.

Many will see ascended masters who were heavy influences on their lives: Jesus, Buddha, Krishna, etc. It is because that is what you expected to see upon your arrival back. That is not to say what you are creating is not real. You are creating it; therefore, it is real.

Let us take someone who believes in nothing. You have lived your life believing there is just nothingness when your body machine shuts down. They will experience that nothingness that they have created for themselves until they are bored of it. At some point they will say to themselves, 'Wait a minute. I'm conscious and aware, so there has to be more than this!' And because they then believe there is more, more will appear. You are creating your experience always.

Another example: if you are brought up in the science world or technology and you believe that is the be all end all, many experience feeling a part of the universe or even creating a living technological city, or even holograms and movie screens. Creating is endless and is everything. There is no wrong or right for it is your experience.

Let us go back to religious followers who believe there is an afterlife of torment and anguish. Because you believe there is this place of fiery damnation, you have the potential to create it when you transition. Some who transition feel immense guilt and fear that they have done something wrong according to their religion that will cause them to be forever punished. Guilt and fear. All energetic frequencies, you see?

They will create that experience. This is not a punishment; this is their own creation. At some point, when their amnesia wears off completely, it will no longer be the experience they wish to have, and they will instantly be removed from that with which they created. They will remember who they truly are.

So, you see, your experience you have after you transition back is whatever experience you want to have. The reason why we are telling you this is so that you can remove the fear. Create something beautiful and exciting instead of something negative and unpleasant.

You will see your soul group again, the group or 'cohort' you are connected with. Your soul family. They will always be there to greet you when you are fully ready to see them again. That really depends on you after you transition. If you believe you will be alone, you will be until you remember you are never alone.

How do you see the spirit realm after you transition? What kind of an experience do you want to have? Because that is ultimately up to you. We suggest not choosing fear while considering this because we do not want you to have a negative experience. However, knowing you are in control of what you are creating is helpful to know for your time on

Earth. No fear of transitioning. You have done it many times before. You are always welcomed home.

As always, we love you very much, dear ones. Thank you for listening."

WHISPER XXX:

The Skeptic

November 4th, 2025

"Hello, dear ones. We are here today to discuss an important topic that sometimes haunts intuitives. Skeptics. Skeptics are those who do not fully believe in intuitive abilities. Here is what we have to say about that:

That is okay.

No one has to believe in anything; however, they will receive the experience they wish to have. What we mean by this is when a skeptic goes into a reading with an intuitive (a tarot and oracle reader, medium, energy healer, psychic, etc.), they are already going in wanting to prove something is not real. They have their mind set on disproving everything.

What kind of frequency is to disprove something? Disproving comes from doubt and doubt is a lower energy vibration. Therefore, with the Law of Attraction, that energy with which is put out will be received in return.

This means that someone going in to prove something is not real will often try to come out with more doubt than they came in – with proof. Even if there was certain evidence during the reading, they will come away with more doubt because the evidence was not to their satisfaction. Would it ever be to their satisfaction? They were expecting evidence so massive and so unreasonable that it would blow their spiritual door wide open.

However, the spirit realm is rarely aggressive in that way; they speak more in gentle whispers than explosions. So, for someone wanting massive, in your face proof, it is just not that way. And just because you want to speak to your mother, it does not mean she will be the one who comes through. You cannot always get what you want; you get what you need.

When someone is going into a reading with the thought, "I am going to prove them wrong. This is not real." Those thoughts of skepticism override any whispers that could have been received. Doubt is often louder than trust because people find it harder to trust than to doubt. So, how can one hear over all that loud, doubt filled static?

The experience with an intuitive will be exactly how the person wants it to be. The more one trusts the process, the more open they are to receive, therefore, their experience will be profound. The less one trusts the process, the more disconnected the experience will be no matter what evidence comes through. Because in the end, what is considered 'good enough'? We are creating our own experience always.

We would also like to add that this is okay. It is not a problem. This was just not the right time for the person to receive the information. They may not have been ready. They may never be ready in this lifetime, and that is okay. People do not have to believe and perhaps they are not meant to. Everyone is on their own separate journey, and everyone will be in a different place in regard to spirituality and what they consider the 'unknown.'

The point here is not to force anyone to believe. One cannot shake someone aggressively and expect results. Give the information gently and move forward. What one may have done is plant a seed. A seed of thought.

Perhaps they will think about the exchange down the line, and they will consider something in a different way. Perhaps an incident in time will spark a remembrance. People do not know the impact they create for another.

For the intuitive, skeptics are great for readers. They force the intuitive to trust the process themselves; forcing them to validate themselves instead of relying on others reactions. It makes the intuitive trust the process from within rather than relying on others to validate for them.

This can be a challenge we understand, but it is necessary. Putting one's own trust in the process externally or outside of themselves is no different than the skeptic wanting proof from external sources. It all comes from within.

Believe wholeheartedly within and nothing can make one doubt themselves or the process again. Everyone is at different points in the growth process; it cannot be expected that everyone is the same. One cannot expect a kindergartner to behave a certain way while sitting through a doctoral course. It cannot be expected.

The bigger truth is the skeptic came to see an intuitive, which means that the skeptic was interested enough to reach out. The skeptic is now curious, and curiosity is the beginning of learning and understanding, learning and understanding leads to remembering and awakening. There are steps; it is not miraculous or instantaneous.

So, although the intuitive may feel the reading was not well received, the skeptic came to the reading in the first place, and a seed was planted. The seed will grow no matter how slowly. One must trust the process as well.

Skepticism is not an obstacle; it is a phase. Every awakened soul has been there. Whether the skeptic notices the seedling planted themselves is not another's responsibility. It is not on someone else. The information was given and released to another, and the transmission was completed.

Release all judgement of the experience. Just allow everything to be exactly where it needs to be at that time, and trust that everything will work out the way it is supposed to. There is always a plan.

We hope this helped anyone that needed to hear this message. And as always, we send you so much love and light. Thank you for listening."

WHISPER XXXI:

Retirement

November 6th, 2025

"Hello, dear ones. It is us once again to discuss a topic human beings talk about frequently: your retirement. Why do we want to speak on this subject today? Because you base your lives on it.

The first thing we would like to address is the fact that you want to retire. Retire is to stop doing. Why do you want to stop doing something? Because you do not enjoy it? Because it takes the energy out of your body without refilling it? Because perhaps you did not enjoy it in the first place?

If you are doing something that does not refill your cup, why are you doing it? Because of money and benefits we assume. We do not understand why humans place dangling carrots in front of each other in order to get results. Because they know the job is not worth doing otherwise. That is very telling.

Without money and benefits there is a lot of fear collectively. This means that you feel you must work for large corporations and sit at a desk all day long wishing you were anywhere but where you actually are. You sit there looking at the clock and watch it tick away.

When this occurs, it is a nudge from us that the pilot light within you is not lit. We say pilot light because it is the driving force within your true being. It is the passion inside of you that makes you excited and fulfilled and joyful.

We ask you to remember that everything is a choice. You are choosing unhappiness due to your fear of lack. The fear that if you do not endure this misery, you will be left with nothing because you feel it provides you with security. However, these corporations have hired you as a number on their payroll, not as an actual person. You are realizing their dreams while you put your dreams aside for after you retire.

This brings us to the point where you actually retire. Many of you feel that your life begins again after you retire. When did your life end before that? People wait to see the world, go out more, live more, love life more after they retire. But here is the thing that you must remember: nothing is guaranteed. There is nothing in any soul contract that your soul must stay here on earth until the contract is up.

This means that waiting to really live till after you retire is not exactly the best decision because nothing is guaranteed. Some contracts are contractually up earlier than retirement age as well. This is because you decided how long you would have this contract last for before you even began your life on earth.

When we say, 'contract is up,' we are speaking about your transition back home. Because of the Law of Forgetfulness, you, yourself, do not remember when your time is up here and when you are coming back home. So, the thought of waiting to begin your life after retirement does not sound like the best point of action.

The whole point of you coming to earth in the first place was to experience everything you could before having to come back home. Within school there are extracurricular activities, correct? Those extracurricular activities are what makes your time on earth truly worth it.

If you are waiting to experience everything for after a certain age, what experiences have you truly had before that? You have waited too long, and instead, you have been unhappy for too long. Misery, fear, and unhappiness are very low frequencies that can affect both your physical body and mind.

Human beings place such interesting limitations on themselves. All for the fear of survival when human survival is never guaranteed. So, what can you do today to begin really living and experiencing?

The first thing we suggest is to get that pilot light inside of the you lit. What passions do you have? What dreams do you think about all the time? What experiences have you always wanted to experience? Now is the time for all of that. If you are sitting at a desk realizing another person's dream, are you living your life or theirs? You call them jobs in human language, but we call them 'callings.'

We, as messengers of light, love our calling. We asked for this because we knew it was something we were passionate about. There is no retirement for us. It is eternal until we feel our calling is complete, which then we rejoin Source. However, Source is ever expanding, so we have eternity to serve you and others. We do not want our jobs to end.

We want the same for you in human form. We want you to find something you are so passionate about that you could never imagine retiring from it. Because it fills your cup and brings you joy. As above so below. You love your callings above, and so you should love your callings below as well. If it is not the case, there is an imbalance. Hence why you are miserable.

We ask that you write down a list of everything that brings you joy and passion. Look at your list. What excites you the most? Reflect on why that excites you the most. What about it makes you excited and happy? This is a list created without fear or lack, so do not allow fear and lack to stop you from writing this list.

Now that you have reflected on it, how can you make something beautiful out of it that can provide that happiness, fulfillment, and security for yourself?

Is that working with animals? Is that helping the homeless? Is that entertaining people and making them laugh? Is it a love for flowers? What is it you have always wanted to do but fear and the fear of lack have stopped you? Because when you do something you love and care about fully, there is no retirement. There is no waiting for fulfillment and happiness. There is no misery because you are always living in that place of happiness and fulfillment, you see?

The reason you are feeling so unhappy and unfulfilled is because you are not meant to be miserable. You are meant to create and experience.

So, instead of dreading your life every single day, get out that figurative match, and get that pilot light inside of you burning again. Because fear and doubt have smothered the flame. Once you are on your correct path, you will see things change in a more beautiful and positive way.

Do not wait to experience life, do it now. Travel to the places you have always wanted to go, go out with friends during the week and have some laughs, go see musicians you love play, go take those fun art classes you have always wanted to take, go dance the night away under the stars, throw fun parties with the ones you love. Experience life now, not later. You will be so much happier that you did.

We hope that you enjoyed this important message, and again, we love you eternally, and we thank you so much for listening."

WHISPER XXXII:

I Am

November 11ᵗʰ, 2025

"Hello, dear ones. We would like you to repeat this to yourself in front of a mirror every day when you wake up and before you go to sleep:

'I am worth it.

I am enough.

I am worthy of all wonderful things.

I am deserving, and I am grateful.

I am extremely important *in* this world.

I am extremely important *beyond* this world.

I am beautiful – inside and out.

I am strength.

I am an incredible, vibrant, loving light.

I am a master creator.

I am love.

I am.'

Because you are. Feel that energetic vibration within your heart. Once you truly feel that within you, that energy bursts outwards in every direction. And, like a magnet, you will draw that same beautiful energy back.

It is time to truly love yourself. Because loving yourself unconditionally is the key. Love is your true power. You deserve happiness, love, and fulfillment. And all of that begins within you.

As always, we are sending you so much love. Thank you for listening."

WHISPER XXXIII:

What Do Angels Look Like?

November 12th, 2025

"Hello, dear friends. We are here to talk about a question many of you have thought about throughout your lives. What do angels look like?

Now again, you have created that term for us, we do not move around calling each other angels, that is just not what we do. We receive a call for help and we answer that call. We are messengers of service. Service being the key word. We are all serving in different ways just as Source serves all of us and vice versa.

But this is about what we look like, not what we do. You go through your lives believing in something or nothing at all. Whatever that belief system is will determine how one sees us. We do not want to startle you when you see us, so being energy, just as you are, we change our appearance to fit the individual experience.

Let us explain using you as an example. When you transition back home, you will have had a lifetime as a human being. That is all you had known in your lifetime, though some do remember other lives elsewhere. So, when you return back home, you will see an imprint of what was. You are always creating the experience you are having, so when you transition, you will be in the form you know best at that time.

This is why you hear many people who have near death experiences say that they saw hands and feet on them or that they were wearing clothes that they loved. It is recreating a memory of your human life so that you are not startled by your true form as an energetic light being. However, once you get acclimated, you, yourself, will remember your true form, and that is what you will then become.

That brings us back to what we look like. Because you are in human form, in order to make our presence less startling, we will often change our form or energy to reflect what you believe. If you are a very religious person and you see us as humans with wings, that is what you will see. If you see us as light beings in our true form, that is what you will see. If you see us as a blue entity that has six heads, that is what you will see.

We assist all beings from all realms, universes, and dimensions. Do you think we appear to them as human beings with wings? They would get startled and confused and more than likely afraid. Why would we startle a being in need of assistance? That sounds counterproductive. Just some humor to lighten the mood. You do not think we have senses of humor? We love humor.

But back to what we look like. This is why we change our form. It is to make your experience with us more relatable so that we can truly help you. You are naturally an untrusting group of beings. Would you accept help from something that looks familiar or something completely different than you? As human beings, you tend to scare easily. We appear as you wish us to appear so that we can continue assisting you when you ask for us.

When Kevin had his Quantum Healing Hypnosis Technique session, he visited us. He saw us in our true, energetic form. This was his decision, even though he is not fully aware he made that choice. But we knew that he would remember us after looking upon us for a moment. He then, indeed, remembered us.

We are very aware of how you are thinking. We can see and hear and feel your thoughts as thoughts are energy. We can read your minds. When you ask for us, you do not have to ask us to look a certain way, we will already know what you need in that moment. Trust.

We hope this helps you to understand us a little better so that you can get to know us again while on this trip through another lifetime. We send you so much love as always, and again, thank you for listening, friends."

WHISPER XXXIV:

The Purpose

November 13th, 2025

"Hello, dear friends, we are back today to talk about this living work of art you have created as well as with others around you. You are not only creators in your own right, but co-creators with the collective.

What does this mean? We will go step by step. Let us take a look at where you are in your life at this moment as well as your lifetimes. Think of everything going on: positively and negatively charged. How did you get to this moment?

Everything has divine timing even when utilizing your free will. Your play has already been written. Your movie has already been shot. You are simply observing it in action. This is because the past, present, and future are all occurring simultaneously. This has already occurred and your soul is simply learning from it.

This means that everything you do in your life has a purpose. It is not even something you need to worry about because you created it before arriving. The plot had been created and the movie had already been filmed. This is why those with premonitions are able to feel what is coming; because it had already occurred. This is because time does not exist in our realm. In fact, when coming back lifetime after lifetime, you will insert yourself in a place and time where you can learn specific lessons.

Let us explain further: picture the history of Earth as a flowing river. When you place yourself on the river, you are propelled forward down it. However, once you get out of the river, you can then place yourself anywhere back into the river as you please: you can walk along the bank towards where you came from and beyond, or you can run up ahead in the direction of the water flow and get back in the water there.

The river was already created. The flow was always in motion. But you can choose where you want to place yourself in that river. Does this make sense?

We will explain even further with your human dates and timelines: let us say you are born in 1935 and after learning all of your lessons, you transition back home in your human year of 1998. Now your soul decides it must learn certain specific lessons and it would be best to be born in 1674, so you place yourself at that part of the river to experience what is necessary to learn those lessons. Then next you jump to your human year of 2893. Different lessons, different part of the river. You place yourself where you will learn those particular lessons the most.

But, why would someone want to regress in human time when everything should be moving forward? It depends on the lessons needed. If you need a lesson on - let us say - the dangers of medieval spirituality, and being forced to keep quiet so that you are not condemned, you will go to a human timeframe that will provide you with that experience. You will not experience that the same way in your current timeline, so one must place themselves on the part of the river that is best for that lesson.

That is an explanation about your multiple lifetimes, but what about why things occur on your current lifetime journey?

In college, Kevin took a class they called "Text Analysis." This was taking a written work, such as a theatrical play, and starting from the end of the play and working their way back to the beginning.

You see the characters at the end of that particular journey and where they were emotionally. But how did they get there? Everything happens for a reason so that a certain lesson can be learned and a certain outcome can be achieved regardless if it takes positive or negative steps to achieve it.

So, take your life where it is right now in your timeline, and do a text analysis with it. You will see the grand design of how you got where you are in the now. You will see that everything had to line up just perfectly for you to be exactly where you are.

Now some may say that they are in a negative place in their life. This is only a transition to get you to the next act of your play. See your life as an observer rather than a victim of circumstance. See that there is possibility for your future even when you cannot see the next part of your path. You are being guided in a direction regardless.

You may not see it now, but the end of this act is coming to an end, and the beginning of the next act is on its way. A new beginning with so many possibilities. Nothing is hopeless. You are exactly where you are meant to be at this moment.

Look back on your own play. See the ups and downs. You have gotten through them all because you are right here reading this. Trust that your own soul has a plan because it has already been written.

The same goes for the collective. What is happening in the world is not coincidence. It is strategic on the part of the collective on a soul level. The final showdown before the happy ending. Consciousness cannot evolve frequency-wise without a frequency to evolve. You coming here to a perfect land without negative choice or problems gives you no room for growth and learning.

Learning is necessary for soul growth. That is the point. If it was not, there would be no point in coming to Earth to have a myriad of experiences. The collective must go through the negative to come out on the other side. How do you know how good things can be if you have never been through pain? It is not pleasant, but it is necessary. Just as you, as an individual, must go through negative experiences, so must the collective as a whole. You are one.

You have heard us before say that Earth is a very challenging school; that you are getting your 'PhDs.' However, you are moving in the right direction. You are seeing what is and what is not working and what is and what is not acceptable for the collective as a whole rather than as individuals. Through this process, Earth will be reborn. A higher frequency dimensional plane of existence.

This is only the beginning. Look back on the hundreds of acts before this collectively; see how things have progressed from one point in your collective's history to another. The collective could never have gotten to this point without the events before it. You are moving forward regardless how negative the world seems in this moment. There has always been progress.

We know this message may be difficult for some to hear, but it is an important one nonetheless. As always, we are sending you so much love, you brave warriors, and thank you for listening."

WHISPER XXXV:

Santarris

November 14th, 2025

"Hello, dear friends. We are here to talk about frequency shifts on your planet. You have all worked very hard to shift the frequency of your planet from 3D to 4D and then eventually to 5D consciousness. Why did this need to happen? And what does it even matter?

The higher the frequency, the closer to Source. Before Earth came to be, there were other planetary systems that were watched as the beings of those planets grew from a low-density planet to one of high density and a collective raise in consciousness.

With this raise in consciousness, there is no need to learn such low vibrational lessons. Lessons such as loving yourself unconditionally, loving others unconditionally, having compassion for everyone and everything, having gratitude always, the realization that you are all one, understanding where you came from, and your Source energy within. This is understood as you raise in frequency. This also means that you will eventually have to shed the physical vessels you have as they will keep you in too low of a vibration.

This does not mean death as death does not exist. You will simply shed your vessels as a collective and stay in that higher vibration on Earth. This is what the universe has been waiting for. But why start each planet in such a low density to begin with?

Lessons and growth. Those souls who wish to ascend at a faster rate must go through the process of fully understanding each and every density. These densities are separate schools created to teach with hands on experience. Some like to call this an experiment. Experiment is such an odd word to us. Experiment almost sounds careless in a way.

We knew what you were capable of, and *we* not only wanted you to prove it to yourselves, but *you* wanted to prove it to yourselves. It is true that we are observing you as you are doing this important work, but that makes it seem as though we are scientists observing lab rats. We do not feel this way.

Without you doing the work, this work would not be accomplished. You are the brave ones selected for this mission. This is a massive mission: to take a low-density planet, which is also a living being itself, and as a collective, raise the energy frequency of the planet from low to high density which can only be done once the collective realizes they are one. This begins with awakening with the truth.

Once the truth is heard it cannot be unheard, and therefore truth spreads until all the collective becomes one once again.

This is not the first time this has occurred. This has happened many times in other galaxies, in other dimensions and realms. Each were given the same tasks, and each rose to higher energetic frequencies. You are not the first, and you will not be the last.

This is all in the name of creation. We are all creators. Source enjoys creating constantly and as we are fractals of Source, we too are creators. The point? Growth. One cannot grow without knowledge and firsthand experience. Growth is the point.

But what happens when Earth becomes a 5D planet of consciousness and challenging lessons and scenarios are no longer learned there? That new planet has already been created. A place of low density with which important, challenging lessons can be learned.

Since you enjoy naming everything, we call this planet Santarris. It has a beautiful mysticism about it, ancient. It has been around for a very long time preparing for the transition where souls can reincarnate and begin their schooling as Earth will no longer be the challenging school it once was.

Santarris will be a place to learn challenging, low frequency lessons where souls can learn and grow so ascension is possible. Does it look like Earth? No. It looks much different. Will you incarnate there? Not likely. As Earth raises in its frequency, you have raised your frequency with it. You are one with the Earth.

By the time you incarnate on Earth as often as you have, and continue to raise your frequency, the thought of regression does not appeal to you. There is no purpose to incarnate there. However, many of you have already chosen to be spirit guides to aid them on their journeys, just as your guides have aided you in the same manner now.

We hope that this message to you was interesting and fun. We love you very much, and we see the difficult work you are doing to raise the frequency on Earth as a collective. Keep up the amazing work, friends. And as always, thank you for listening."

WHISPER XXXVI:

Ghosts

November 15ᵗʰ, 2025

"Hello again, dear friends. We are here to talk about a subject many of you fear: ghosts. You fear them because you have watched many movies telling you to fear them.

But here is what they truly are. They are energy. Just as you are energy and trees are energy and air is energy and light is energy. Like attracts like. The energy you are giving out you will receive in different ways.

So, how does this make sense when it comes to ghosts or as you call poltergeists that are able to move things around your house or cause a ruckus. When you know that these beings are energy, you realize you have much more power than you believe you do. You are giving the energies too much power over you.

A 'ghost' as you call them are energetic beings just as you are, however, they chose not to return home due to something that is keeping them on this Earthly plane. They are not souls that are necessary lost, but more like energies that are still attracted to living human lives for different reasons.

For example, while here in human form, they owned a business that they worked for their entire human life. Nothing in the world mattered as much as this business.

Since you cannot take the business with you, there is a stubbornness present. Who will take care of their 'baby'? How could anyone replace them because only they know how to do it correctly?

Another example: someone is an addict of some kind, and they transition to their true form, however, because the amnesia of living as a human is still fresh, they will attempt to find those of the same frequency to feed off of energetically. However, this will not last forever as the 'ghost' as you call them will eventually realize they cannot have an actual human experience without being human, and therefore travel home after that realization.

That brings us back to hauntings. If you are experiencing a negative entity within your home or following you from place to place, there is a reason. Oftentimes it is the energy given by the human beings themselves that is attracting the energy of the same kind. What you do not realize is that all people have energies of all kinds coming in and out of your homes and all around you. The difference is that the frequency you are at will attract those of the same frequency. Like a magnet.

This means that if you are at your most joyful and love fills within you, the energies surrounding you will be those that match your vibration. If you are angry or depressed or an addict, you will attract those of the same frequency to you. This means if a place such as a home holds a certain frequency, an energy of that frequency will be attracted to it. This is why you have hauntings within places and hauntings around people. There are also hauntings that are due to negative events as well, which is residual negative energy.

If you ever notice why many bars or pubs are haunted, it is because of the vibration within it. Alcohol is poison. Everyone within the building is poisoning themselves willingly. That type of low frequency immediately attracts energies of the same frequency which tend to be lower vibrationally.

You may ask, how can a nonphysical entity pick up physical objects and toss them across the room? Again, it is energy. The stronger the energy frequency being generated by the human being, the more intense it gets. This means that the more angry or more depressed you are, the stronger the energy that is given off from you. The one giving the entity all that power is you.

This is important for you to understand because this gives you your power back. Knowing you control what comes around you due to frequency means that you can fix it yourself. Change your frequency. Raise it higher and higher. If something negative is in your life, change it. You hold the power. You are much stronger than you think you are in this physical form. Take your power back.

If you have an addiction, the entity is attached to you because they were more than likely an addict as well. They are attached because they are vicariously living through your experience. They want to feel that high. They want to have that experience, you see? Once the addict gets the help they need, and the frequency is raised, there will no longer be the low frequency energy to supply it, and it will move on.

The way to free yourself from the negative energy around you is to change the energy within you. You will see a change.

If it is a 'ghost' that is connected to a specific place because it was important to them in their human life, you simply must tell them that you have everything taken care of, that they do not need to worry, and that they can choose to fully transition without any concern. Politely ask it to leave. If that does not work, you may need assistance from an intuitive who can directly communicate and help them.

We hope that this message helps you to understand. Do not fear. Take your power back. We love you so much, and as always, thank you for listening."

WHISPER XXXVII:

Rejoining Your Soul Group

November 17th, 2025

"Hello, dear friends. Have you missed us? We are back to discuss a topic that was asked of us: when you go back home after your transition will you see your family members such as your father and mother and siblings?

The answer is more complicated than just saying 'yes.' It is a 'yes, *and* –' type of situation. Let us explain so that it is clear. Before arrival into this simulation, you agreed to have this experience so that you could learn and grow. This is what we have discussed in previous messages to you.

However, in order to be fully immersed into the experience, you also agreed to have a temporary amnesia of sorts that would prevent you from fully remembering where you truly came from.

As you recall in a past message, not having this amnesia would cause you to have immense homesickness, and would probably be the cause of frequent fatalities. So, you understand how that would not benefit you or those around you who need to learn specific lessons or finish specific missions that were agreed upon before your arrival.

At the end of this specific lifetime, and you transition from your physical form, the amnesia takes some time to wear off. This means that if you are not fully aware of what is happening, you will look down and see hands and feet. You will see arms and legs. You will feel, in a way, semi-human at that point; almost an echo of what was.

We are all very aware that this occurs because we have seen it all before. This is very usual in these moments. Since you are creating your own experience, what happens next is created by you and your soul group. Your soul group are the souls that you have moved through existence with. They are souls who have incarnated with you many, many times throughout eternity assisting each other with lessons and missions.

Your soul group or soul family are well aware of your state of consciousness: still half in the human realm and half in spirit. In order for you not to become shocked by the experience, your soul group will appear to you as you knew them in that particular lifetime; just the same as we spoke, in a previous message, about how angels will appear as whatever you think they should appear as in your mind.

This means that you will see your mother and father or partners or siblings or friends or whoever they were in your lifetime as they were in life. They will appear to you in this form as to avoid any unnecessary shock. We want this to be a pleasant and exciting and joyful experience.

There will be much celebration of your return because coming to Earth is no easy task. You are so brave to have wanted to volunteer for such a mission. After a while, the amnesia of what was dissipates, and you will fully remember who and what you are. This means you will remember your true energetic light form.

Once you remember what you truly are, you will see your soul family in the same way; as members of your adoring cohort all working together to assist each other through lifetimes. So, will you see your family and friends again when you transition?

Yes, and once the amnesia fully wears off, you will see your soul family in their true form. Not as parents or children or spouses, but as fellow travelers, equals, teammates, classmates all working towards the same goal together. It is a much deeper love and connection than you have ever felt in your lifetimes on Earth.

This means that you have nothing to be worried about. You will see all of your beloved family, because they truly are your family. They are your family and friends all at once, and you have known them all for eternity. And that is a beautiful thing indeed.

As always, we love you so much, and we thank you for listening, dear friends."

WHISPER XXXVIII:

World Division

November 20th, 2025

"Hello, dear friends. We are here today to speak to you about the collective and the division you have created from the beginning of human time. Human beings tend to make everything about division. Who you are, what you do, where you live, what you look like. This is because of the low density on your planet. The lower the density, the further away from Source.

This is not your fault. It is part of the evolution of your planet. The great experiment created to see if human beings are able to rediscover themselves and awaken not only within themselves but as one with the collective. This was not an easy challenge, but you were so gracious and brave to volunteer for this.

Through your human years, through the river of lifetimes we have mentioned before, you have gone through thousands of human years of evolution. You have started at the lowest density possible and have worked your way upward. What does this mean?

As we have stated: the lower the density the farthest from Source. Look back even a thousand years ago in human years. What was occurring? If you consider the violence that occurred then and look where it is now, would you say there has been an improvement? We would say yes. There has been an improvement.

The higher the frequency the closer to Source, the closer to Source the more access to information. Notice as the collective's frequency raised, technology was created, ideas were born, art thrived. If you are in too low of a vibration energetically, these ideas would not be possible or even thought of. Because creating is a type of channeling. The collective works as a whole not as individuals.

The higher the vibration, the more positive changes can occur. The more realizations are had. You are noticing this now. These conversations would never have happened before because people were killed if they spoke of these spiritual matters. Witchcraft they called it; those who had premonitions or could speak to those in the spirit realm.

Many intuitives were 'removed' from society out of fear of being possessed or evil. It all stemmed from fear. Humans tend to destroy that with which they do not understand. Now, in your current human year, you are able to have these conversations more freely without persecution in most places. Progress comes with higher frequency.

Back to division. Yes, it is true that we digress often, but in order to get to the main topic at hand, we need to explain how things work so that there is better understanding of it.

Division is created because human beings see themselves as individuals only, rather than the whole. Since you see yourselves as separate from each other there is a need to control and conquer selfishly. Greed is the main culprit which stems from the fear of lack. If you feel you can never have enough, you will take what is not yours out of sheer panic of not having enough. But when is enough enough? It never is. This is what creates your divide.

Many human years ago human beings decided to take what was not theirs because they wanted to conquer the entire world. But the world is not one person's to conquer. The Earth itself is its own living entity. It cannot be owned. You simply have the privilege to live amongst its beauty.

So, where is the human race going in the future in regard to all of the division? As human time continues moving forward down the river of time, you will see much less division. There will not be states or countries as you see them today. It will become one. It will be about community. Working as a whole because everyone will realize they are all one with each other. There will not be any war or violence because that which affects one affects the whole. Therefore, division is no longer a desired outcome.

You will no longer judge others based on appearance, because you will realize that you are all having this experience together as one. Because you are one collectively. This is when you all will transition from physical form to your true form as light beings. Evolution.

You may think this process will take forever, but it will not. Look back at your collective's history from this moment, and work your way backwards. Your frequency as a collective is rising faster than ever before.

Just look at the last two hundred years alone. Two hundred years ago, from this moment in your time, was extremely different. No human made machines were flying through the air, no one was driving gas powered cars, no electricity in the home, no one had air conditioning, less rights for people in general, people treated everyone worse than they do in your current time.

In two hundred years, you have managed to raise the frequency of the collective so much that you are in a much better place than the human race has ever been. This does not mean that it is still not challenging. There is still much work to be done. But the point is that the work *is* being done, and things are shifting in a positive direction.

To continue moving into a higher frequency, you must all see the cracks in society. You must see problems within your governments and religions and other institutions. That is where there is much discomfort. But as the collective awakens to their oneness, these societal institutions will dissolve. All must see the cracks in the system as one for there to be a major change as a whole. This is what is occurring now.

The collective is seeing what they will and will not tolerate anymore. They are seeing that in order to look out for yourself, you must look out for your fellow neighbors, because helping your fellow neighbor, in turn, helps you. It benefits everyone. You are moving slowly out of the division phase and you will be moving into your oneness. It is an exciting time.

This cannot be done forcefully; however, it is a gentle shift. Be the change you want to see in the world. That energy will spread. If done forcefully, you will be met with different results. Negative results. As your time passes, you will see these shifts in frequency accelerate because you cannot stop this train. The wheels are already in motion.

We know that this can feel extremely uncomfortable. Giving birth is not comfortable, but the end result is beautiful. You are birthing the new world as a collective, and you are feeling all the contractions. But it is a labor of love, and you will see the beauty when it is done.

We ask you to watch what is occurring not as victims of circumstance, because that will keep you in a negative frequency, but as an observer; an observer watching the collective shift to a higher frequency than ever seen before on this planet.

You are creating this beautiful, magnificent shift in consciousness. You are doing incredible things. Trust the process no matter how challenging it can be. Everything is occurring at the right time. The shift is happening.

We hope that this message helped you. And as always, we are sending you so much love and light, and we thank you so much for listening."

WHISPER XXXIX:

The Frequency of Gratitude

November 26th, 2025

"Hello, dear friends. We are here today to talk about the importance of gratitude. Many people live in the frequency of lack. You think about everything that you do *not* have rather than everything that you *do* have.

Why is this important? Because if you live in a frequency of lack, you are not living at your fullest. You are living wishing you had more rather than appreciating what you have already received. You are not living in the now.

Gratitude is a very high energy frequency. With living in a place of gratitude, you realize you have been gifted so many beautiful things: a roof over your head, a means of transportation, security, loving family and friends near you, love for yourself, a healthy relationship, your health, a direction you feel pulled to go on your journey, etc. You may not have everything we have mentioned in this moment, but you have one or more of the above.

When people think of abundance, they often think of money immediately. Money are pieces of paper or metal that you have placed on a pedestal above you. This means that these low energy objects control you energetically because you allow them to control you. You have placed them on this pedestal yourself because society tells you to. When you want an abundance of money when is it enough? When do you have enough of it?

It is very rare that you do have enough of it because once you have money, the next want is for more. The more money the happier some feel they will be. Or the more money the more secure and safe they will feel.

But if you can never have enough money, when do you become happy? When do you become safe and secure? At what point are you satisfied? At what point will these monetary objects bring you joy? Because the moment that you receive money, you immediately fear losing it. More fear is placed within. If you do not have enough money, there is a fear of lack; when you feel you finally have enough, there is a fear of losing it, which stems from the fear of lack.

Happiness does not come from objects but emotional connectivity. What is the money bringing you and focus on that. Is it security and stability? Adventure? Closer to your purpose and what excites you? Notice how these we have mentioned are high frequency energies. It is not the objects that you are reaching for, it is your inner fulfillment and passion. When focusing on higher frequency wants and desires, you are telling the universe you want more of it, and the money will follow.

At what point does having an abundance of money turn into greed? The frequency shifts from negative to even more negative quickly. Being a very low energy frequency, greed can make people do very selfish things for their own benefit while harming others. It is all about intention.

What energy are you putting forth when asking for abundance? To say that you are desperate for money is living in a place of lack. Lack is a low energy frequency, therefore, you will bring more lack into your life. You get back what you have put out into the universe.

It is time to live in the frequency of gratitude. With gratitude, you are not wishing for more, you are grateful for what you have. If you are grateful for what you have, you are already whole, living in the frequency of abundance; you are not living in fear or anger or desperation. Since you already feel you are abundant, and you are grateful for that abundance, you will attract more abundance to you due to the frequency you are emanating.

This is about shifting your thinking so that you can get more of the positive things you want in your life. If you are living in lack, you will receive that frequency; if you are living in abundance, you will receive that frequency. This is entirely up to you. It is all intention. You are not waiting to be completed; you are already complete.

When you speak of the abundance you are grateful for in your life, it comes from a place of appreciation, gratitude, and love. This will take you a long way. We ask that you look within your heart, recognize everything you have in your life no matter what it is, and do not focus on what you do not have in your life. This is about changing your mindset to help you in this present moment.

We ask that you create a gratitude list that you can read to yourself before bed every night and when you wake up in the morning. Read the list and feel everything you are reading within your heart. Close your eyes. Envision each thing you have written. Feel that loving warmth fill your body. More abundance will follow.

We hope that this message has helped you, and we want you to know that we love you very much, and we are always rooting for you. Thank you for listening, dear friends."

WHISPER XL:

Spiritual Disconnect

December 2nd, 2025

"Dear friends, we are here today to speak on the topic of feeling disconnected spiritually. There come many points in time when you feel you do not hear us, you do not think we are present with you anymore. Where you have heard us so clearly for long periods of time and then it seems as though it abruptly stops.

The first thing we want to remind you of is that you are never disconnected. You cannot be disconnected because you are the connection. You are the creator of this experience; therefore, you cannot be disconnected from it. You are it. We are a part of your experience just as you are a part of our experience. We are one and oneness can never be separated.

There are reasons why you are feeling, what you consider, disconnected. The first is a lower frequency shift and another is you are being prepared for a higher frequency shift. Some say that frequency shifts can feel out of control and chaotic, but true frequency shifts are gradual and soft.

If a shift is forced by other means such as substance abuse, emotional trauma, or psychedelics, this is when the frequency shifts can feel loud and forced and uncomfortable. However, no one experience is alike. But many shifts occur within the silence.

How do you know in which direction you are shifting? This can be understood by the energy within you currently. What is occurring in your life at this moment? Are you going through more complicated or trying times? Or are you in a place of contentment and joy? Energy is always shifting in one direction or another. Regardless of what direction you are going into, we are still guiding you, you are never alone.

When your energy is shifting to a higher frequency, there will be pockets of human time when you may feel that disconnect still. You will have soft periods where you do not understand what is happening. As we mentioned before, these shifts are soft and calm.

Your human body is being prepared for this change. If it is too abrupt, it can feel like you are completely out of control of your own self, and that can feel scary. This is not a desired experience. Therefore, these shifts occur in the calmness, the lightness.

What is happening during these shifts? The higher your frequency gives you access to more information. We have mentioned before that the higher the frequency the closer to Source, therefore, the higher the frequency the more access to higher-self and Source information and what you would call downloads. This can sound like ringing in your ears at times when we are giving you information to process. This can also sound like silence as we upgrade your system.

What type of upgrades are we speaking of? As you raise your frequency, your natural born ethereal abilities become stronger. Your third eye opens wider, things come more into focus than before. Information you may not have been able to hear or see or feel before is suddenly accessible. This is what we consider upgrades to your human system. Everyone has these features within them; it just depends when and if you have chosen to tap into them within your current lifetime.

In order for this to occur, your human body must be prepared for it. Too much at once can cause an energetic overload which can have a crippling effect, and that is not the intention here. The desired outcome is for this process to happen gradually over the span of human months or even years depending on how far along you are in your schooling. The more advanced you are in your schooling, the shorter these downloads take to process because you remember.

If it takes longer for you, do not get frustrated. You will get there eventually. Patience is key as this is a process that cannot be forced. Patience is very important. Therefore, there may be a month here and there where you will feel as though nothing is happening with your natural gifts. You will feel as though we are harder to hear, harder to connect with even during meditation. You may not feel drawn to access your gifts as frequently as you did before. It may even feel like you are regressing, but you are not. You are being prepared.

Take this time for self-care. Do not beat yourself up over this because you are always progressing. You are always progressing because that is the entire point of this experience. If you are not progressing there is no point, and there would be no purpose to all of this. But there is always purpose to everything.

Know that deep within your heart center. Trust the process even when you feel you have nothing to trust. You are not doing anything wrong. You are being prepared for the next phase. You are not lost; you are exactly where you are supposed to be at this very moment.

So, if you go into a period where you are feeling a bit lost and you are not sure what is going on, refer back to this message, and know that you are not lost at all. You are just in a transitional state as you step into the next phase of your life.

Thank you for listening to this message, and we hope this helps you. We love you very much, and we are always with you no matter what. Trust."

WHISPER XLI:

Intolerance

December 3rd, 2025

"Hello, dear ones. We are back at this moment to discuss what many of you see in the world: intolerance. Where does intolerance come from? It comes from a lack of understanding. Without understanding or the attempt to understand, judgement is placed on the subject in question.

Human beings are notorious for having intolerance. You allow others to tell you how to think rather than thinking for yourself. When this occurs, you tend to go along with the herd. Almost like lemmings heading for an unseen cliff but trusting what the majority is doing rather than looking ahead and seeing the cliff and making a decision for yourself.

This is an extreme example, but it is an important one. You have religions, governments, society in general, who often tell people what to think. What is acceptable, who is acceptable, where is acceptable, when is acceptable. This trickles down to the rest of the people who look up to these institutions for guidance. This then spreads to people they know and so on. The toxic waters cascade downward.

The important fact is without the listening audience; those institutions do not have any power over others. They must get you to believe what they feel is truth so they can keep that power, and they desperately need it. Notice how their stories change as time goes on. They must adapt in order to keep their power. One day they say one thing, the next they say another, and their beliefs change faster than they change their socks.

At what point do the people listening begin to question? Why is following the herd more important than having your own thought? Is it easier? Does it leave you less accountable? Are you afraid of how others will perceive you? Intolerance often turns to hatred because of the refusal to understand. When others are trying to be their true selves, even though they are not harming anyone in the process, they are treated as cockroaches that must be squashed out of society. Intolerance stems from the refusal to put the shoe on the other foot.

If you look at someone who is different than you in any way, you must place yourself in their shoes. What are they going through? Why does society look down on them? Why does this affect you so much? *Does* it truly affect you? Where does this intolerance stem from? Why do you care so much that it upsets you? How would you feel if you were the one people were focused on in a negative way? What if others saw *you* as the cockroach that needed squashing? This creates an understanding which in turn creates tolerance of others rather than the opposite effect. Self-reflection.

Another example on a different level: if your partner has low self-confidence in themselves, and they must always ask for reassurance on every decision. This can be frustrating for the partner who does not understand why their partner always needs reassurance. Instead, it is an annoyance. This is because there is a lack of understanding and empathy. Everything happens for a reason. A constant need for reassurance stems from low self-esteem and self-confidence. This low self-confidence also stems from childhood or a traumatic event.

If you begin to understand where the other person is coming from, there is then an understanding where instead of getting frustrated or angry with the person always needing reassurance, there is compassion instead. An understanding, you see?

This concept of understanding should be used in any instance where you might get a negative feeling towards another. Why is this happening? And would you like this same treatment done to you? If you would not want that same treatment, then you must reach an understanding internally.

Why are you so affected by it? Would you like to be treated in this manner? Is this your own personal thought or something taught to you by others, external conditioning? Does this person or persons force you to see yourself in a way that scares you deep in your shadow? Self-reflection is so important. You cannot grow without it. You are capable of understanding and compassion. Think with your heart.

We hope our message has helped you today, and we thank you so much for listening. We love you, dear friends."

WHISPER XLII:

Sexual Identity

December 4ᵗʰ, 2025

"Hello, dear friends. We are here to discuss the topic of sexuality on Earth. It is interesting to us that you focus so heavily on this subject as though it truly matters. It does not.

Did you know that when it comes to sexuality on other planets or planetary civilizations this is not discussed or cared about in the way that you have brought it to the forefront of conversations?

On other planets there are more sexual orientations than you have letters, and it is just known and appreciated and discussed positively rather than condemning those who may be different from what you consider 'the norm.'

What is the norm? The norm is created by those in power who wish for everyone else to live a life in their own image rather than based on the individuals. The problem is, these ideologies have stuck around for thousands of years.

In order to make yourselves believe someone is different from the others is to say that it is a trauma response or a mental illness rather than it being who they truly are. In ancient times, people who were considered different were actually revered, often considered the chosen ones. Now even that is too far in the other direction.

People who are different than you should not be condemned or revered but that it just is. We are all one. You are playing out every experience possible in the human experience. That means that all of you, at one point or another, have been all genders, all races, all nationalities, and yes, all sexual identities. You have been them all. So, while condemning others you are truly condemning yourselves. What are you supposed to do with this information?. Treat people who are different than you respectfully. Let it be. It is natural. In fact, other sexualities in the galaxy you currently reside would probably make your head spin and question everything you have been living in your lifetime.

But you see, it does not matter. Everyone is different. Sexuality is fluid, it is ever changing, ever evolving. That is the beauty of the human experience, not a negative thing about the human experience. Not all of you are meant to have children. It was never the intention for all to give birth. If you did, your planet would be extremely overpopulated more than it is now. This human experience is about connection. That is what this is about. So, it does not matter what your gender is or is not. Are you connecting with another? How is this connection making your life more enjoyable and fulfilled? As long as you are not harming another or yourself, that is all that matters.

We see political and religious systems who base large portions of their beings trying to turn people against each other so that they can remain in power. That is all that this is about and all it ever has been about. But you are slowly coming out of your comas. You are seeing the truths. You are understanding more and more.

Do not be exclusive, be inclusive. Embrace the people next to you who may be different. Because you were never meant to all be the same. You are each a mirror to each other. You show each other your differences because that is what makes you, you. Because in other lifetimes you have also been considered the 'other.' You are creators of your own experience, and you are all extensions of Source.

Since you were all created from Source which is no gender, you have that creativity inside of you to explore all genders, all possibilities, all experiences.

No more exclusion, no more finger pointing at those who are different than you. No more treating others terribly because others have told you to in the name of religion or government or family members, etc.

Have discussions that matter such as inclusion, gratitude, love, compassion, tolerance, serving others, etc. If those were the topics focused on, Earth would be a completely different place.

But it all must start somewhere, and it is at this point in the river of your time that it begins. It all starts with you.

We hope that this message has helped those who needed to read it. We thank you so much for listening, and we love you very much."

WHISPER XLIII:

Exit Points

December 5th, 2025

"Hello, dear ones. We are back to discuss the topic of exit points. Now we understand that many people have triggering issues surrounding the topic of transitioning from this realm to the next, so if that triggers you, we do not want to create a negative response, and so we ask for you to move passed this message.

Let us first say that transitioning from this realm to the next is completely natural and there is nothing to fear as you have done this many times over lifetimes and lifetimes. This may sound exhausting, but it really is not when considering there is an eternity.

This experience is not new by any means. You remember how to come into your body just before birth, and you remember how to exit the body when transitioning back from the human experience.

If you think of your human experience like a virtual reality experience, it feels very real to you at the time. You see your three-dimensional surroundings, but instead of only seeing and hearing, you have all the senses during. Each 'game' is catered to the individual depending on what they would like to learn in that specific experience. We have already discussed in past messages how this occurs, so we will move forward to our actual point.

During your individualized simulation, your higher self has several moments where you can decide you have had enough of the experience and end the 'game.' We are speaking in virtual reality terms, which is why we used the word 'game.'

You are experiencing one of the most difficult and challenging simulations that your higher self can experience, so there must be measures and plans in place that can get you out of the experience at certain points.

During those specific moments, your higher self can choose to continue or end the experience at that moment. Why is this opportunity given to your higher self? Because if certain lessons learned or taught are completed, if there is nothing else needed from that specific lifetime, the experience can be ended.

It is true that each individual decides how and when they will transition, and the same goes for the exit points throughout the simulated experience as well. Have you ever almost gotten into an accident of some kind and your response was, 'I almost died?' Or you were having a terrible asthma attack, and nothing is helping, but suddenly you come around? Those moments that leave you guessing if you almost did not make it through a certain event were exit point moments.

Those moments that happen throughout one's human lifetime are the points where your soul can make the decision to continue onward or end the experience at that point. But what feels like a split second to you is actually timeless in the spirit realm. The simulation stops momentarily until the higher-self, along with their guides and light council, can make the appropriate decision. Essentially the simulation experience is placed on a brief hold.

During this time you all discuss the benefits of continuing onward in the experience or if you have accomplished your goals of learning and teaching specific lessons, how ending the simulation will affect others' simulated experiences based on their own goals and lessons that need to be learned and taught. A lot of careful thought is placed in this decision and is not taken lightly.

Once the decision is made, the experience is fixed to have that specific outcome. For example: Kevin was driving on the expressway once, and a traffic jam occurred on the off ramp. This semi-truck came flying towards him without a way to stop. This was one of his exit points.

What are the benefits of staying? What lessons or teachings are still left to be learned and taught? Kevin's higher self, guides, and council decided it would be best for Kevin to continue his simulation, and so we forced the semi-truck to stop just before hitting him, which Kevin thought was impossible at the time.

So, you see? Everyone has these moments, and they are nothing to fear. Everything is always working out for your highest good. There is nothing you need to do with this information other than to trust that your higher self, your guides, and council are always on your side and are always with you at every moment.

This is also to help you understand this experience you are currently living as well since it can often feel very confusing or frustrating at times. We understand this. Know you are exactly where you are supposed to be at this very moment. Trust.

We hope that you found this message interesting, and we thank you very much for listening. We love you dearly, friends."

WHISPER XLIV:

The Source Within

December 6th, 2025

"Hello, our dear friends. We come today to talk about your true inner power; who you truly are, and where you come from. It is an exciting message that Kevin has spoken about in his own messages once before. The fact that you are Source. Let us explain this so that it is more understandable and not confusing.

Look at your Creator, your Source. Look what it has created to explore all possibilities, all energies, all types of consciousness, all connections. The multi-dimensional universes and realms it has created and cared for were all created from its beautiful and eternal energy.

What was the point? To create and live what has been created. Through creation comes understanding and growth. Our Source is eternally growing because it is absorbing all the firsthand information that we are all providing.

Knowing about something is completely different than having fieldwork experience, and therefore, the fieldwork experience begins with all of us. The fractals.

That shows you the power of our Source. But as people have said before, all beings have been created in its likeness, which is a hundred percent true. What does this mean? Source is a brilliant ball of loving and creative and beautiful energy. Excited for more creating and more learning; an ongoing journey for the Divine. It is not about religions or bowing down to Deities.

This is where you must have your open minds and hearts ready. If you are not ready to hear this information, perhaps you should move onto another message. We love and thank you.

This is where we get even more excited to talk to you. Where does Source come from? If we are all a part of a Source ourselves, where does our Source come from? Energy cannot be created or destroyed, correct? However, energy comes from other energy sources.

This means that it is true that these universes, realms, and dimensions are all from the same incredible being, however, our Source is the offspring of another that for our sake of this teaching we will call Mega-Source. And that Mega-Source is the offspring of what we will call an Ultra-Source. They simply cannot be named because there are infinite Sources that go on and on and on. There is no beginning and there is no end.

It is like Russian dolls where you have a larger doll, and inside it is another doll and then another and another. Except there is no end and no beginning for eternity.

Everything is a fractal of something else. Everything. Nothing can just create itself, it was already created, you see?

What does this mean for you? Since you come from an eternal lineage of Sources, you, yourself, are Source. You are your own Source, your own creator. And just as your own Source created you in its own image, you are creating in your own image. You are a beautiful energetic, creative, light Source. What does this mean?

You are a fractal of your higher self. You are a creator of your own universes and realms and dimensions just as your Source has done the same and so on. That is what lives within you now. You are more powerful and creative and wondrous than you could ever imagine.

Trust and believe in your incredible power. As you are learning and growing in the name of our Source, others are learning and growing in the name of you.

This does not mean to have a big head about it as it is natural. However, it is to understand the process that you are not some forgotten entity floating around somewhere. You are infinitely important. You are each Sources born of the same Source. You are all family in oneness. Because the oneness is truly infinite.

Feel your own power within. Be the creator you truly are. You are worthy and special and loving and creative. All of that lives within you. Trust and believe because it is truth.

We hope that this post empowers you and helps you to understand how beautiful and infinite and loving and powerful you are. We love you so much. And as always, thank you for listening, friends."

WHISPER XLV:

The Whole Truth

December 12th, 2025

"Hello, friends. We are here to talk about a subject that is very important. There are many out there who are telling people that their way is the only truth and others are wrong.

You are forgetting that you are each a creator of your own reality. So, there is no right or wrong when all things are true. We have discussed this many times in past transmissions before, but we feel the need to say this again for the people in the back. You are the creator of your own reality. You live what is true to you not someone else's truth and reality.

For someone to tell you that something is not true or not real when it is true and real in your heart tells you that those people are not as spiritually awakened as they scream to others from their rooftops.

Remember that spirituality is quiet and gentle not forceful and unkind. The truth is what you believe as long as you are not harming others in the name of your beliefs.

When one feels the need to comment and berate someone for their views, they are practicing their own spirituality and pushing it onto others in ways of bullying, much like it was done for thousands of years to those who were persecuted for being different.

For those trying to bully others into their own views are no different. So, you see, there is no difference. A bully is a bully is a bully. It does not matter if physical violence is used or not, because words are just as powerful energetically.

What does this mean for you? Believe what you feel is true in your heart center. It is your higher self's central hub. If you trust in something within your own heart you cannot be wrong. If you wish to believe in Santa Claus, believe in Santa Claus because that is your reality and your truth. You are creating that magic. Even if it is just to feel the true magic that is around you at certain parts of the year, then trust in it and go with it.

Being young at heart and being creative is what living this experience is all about, and those who tell you otherwise are in a completely different part of their own journey. Some choose to live in fear. And yes, that is a choice.

You will always have those people who will try to make you second guess yourself or not believe in yourself or make you afraid in someway. This is done out of their own fears and insecurities.

Why fear? They must get others to believe what they believe due to feeling isolated, and fear is an easy tactic used from the beginning of the human species. They need others to listen because they feel alone in their own belief systems, and they fear opening their minds to new possibilities.

So, those who tell you you are incorrect and bully you for your beliefs are simply afraid of opening their own minds to other possibilities due to their own belief systems.

What to take away from this message to you: trust your own belief systems; ones that are positive and not harmful to you or others. Keep an open mind to new ideas you may never have considered before, do not try or attempt to get people to change their own beliefs.

You can share your truth to see if it resonates with others, but that is as far as it needs to go. It does not enter a bullying or manipulative stage at all. Again, spirituality is quiet and gentle not forceful, manipulative, or fear based.

You are creating your own experience, and that means your beliefs are your own. They are special to you because you created it. For example: If you fear your friends from other planetary systems are out to harm you, that is the reality you are living in. If you feel your galactic friends are here to work with you side by side in friendship and trust, that is the reality you are living. This goes with every aspect of life.

Another example: if one intuitive is telling you that using different tools such as tarot, crystals, pendulums, etc. are silly and moronic, yet you use them with much success, how is your way wrong? It is not. There is no wrong. They are called divination tools for a reason. Everyone is different, and no experience is the same. Trust your own way because it is your own. Others are simply trying to make you doubt yourself due to their own insecurities.

Listen to those who share their stories. See what resonates with you and what does not resonate with you. Take the information that resonates and apply it to your creative experience. Things that do not resonate, remove from your thoughts.

Do not put fear into others because you have fear yourself. State what you believe and let others decide whether they have the same belief or not. That is where it ends. No condemning, no insulting, no manipulating. Trust in your own belief system and go with the flow.

We hope that this message has helped you, and as always, we love you very much. Thank you for listening."

WHISPER XLVI:

The Shift

December 16th, 2025

"Hello, dear ones. We are here today to talk to you about what is occurring in your world currently. You are noticing the big shift. The cleansing. The awakening of your planet. But, as always, it is not comfortable at the very beginning. It can be extremely uncomfortable and challenging.

As the world begins to shift as a collective, it often becomes more aware of the frequency it is moving out of. When people fight change, meaning frequency in this case, the world can struggle in many ways.

There is no stopping the frequency shift, but the more people resist change in an attempt to maintain control, the more intense things can feel. Some become desperate to keep things as they are rather than moving forward. This often happens in the name of control, because moving forward means less control of individuals and a greater remembering of the collective as a whole. Because we are one.

Collective shifts tend to occur when many are witnessing the same challenges at the same time. This is why major changes often follow major world events, because the entire world is paying attention together. The timing and outcome of this shift depend on the collective as a whole.

This time you are living in now is a period of significant transition. One of the largest shifts in planetary frequency is beginning to unfold. This is why many of you felt called to be here at this time. You have lived many lifetimes preparing for moments such as this. You each carry unique missions that involve raising the frequency of this planet.

That means helping people who need assistance, being kind to those around you, and choosing to be the change you wish to see in the world. Embody it. Be a bright light so that others may find their way through the darkness. Remember that this work is done gently, with inclusion and great care, not with violence or exclusion. You must stay in a higher frequency. Do not spread the fear.

You are part of the beginning of great change. You have been preparing for this work for lifetimes. Stay strong, and stay together as one. Even in difficult moments, meaning can be shaped by how you choose to respond.

As always, we love you very much. We are so proud of you, and we admire your incredible bravery and courage. Thank you for listening."

WHISPER XLVII:

Puzzle Pieces

December 19th, 2025

"Hello, dear friends. You have heard us before discuss the topic of raising frequency about not only as an individual but as a collective, and this stems from that discussion. We have mentioned on an individual level about purpose and how when you are not on track, you may notice things in your life going in a very challenging direction.

The same goes for the collective. The issue here is that you see yourselves as separate from each other. This is where you are mistaken. You come from the same Source. You are extensions of the Divine.

This means you are one, not separate. However, you have collectively agreed to forget about all of this to see if it is possible to remember and put the pieces back together.

We do not consider the lives you are living as a game, but we will use a game analogy for this moment. The name of the game is to remember. But in order to remember fully, one's frequency must raise so that you are more connected to your Source energy. The further away you are frequency wise from Source energy, the less you remember, and the less likely you are to believe in what you truly are.

Now, back to the game analogy. You are finding your purpose as human beings, correct? You are constantly shifting, trying to figure out what works and what does not. Not only are you doing this within one specific lifetime, but you are doing this over the course of all of them.

With that as an individual, one must apply that same concept to the collective. As the frequency naturally shifts into a higher state, those who walk amongst its beauty must also shift in order to remain on the planet. You are continually shifting frequencies regardless if you realize it or not. It is a natural progression.

The trick, as a collective, is that you must all build the puzzle together as one entity rather than billions of separate individuals. What is this puzzle? The puzzle of remembering who you truly are as one. This is not an easy task by any stretch of the imagination, because in order to complete a puzzle as one, you must think as one.

It has taken you lifetimes to understand this, but you are finally at the beginning of this oneness that we have been speaking of. You may feel out of sorts at the moment with intense emotions across your planet, but that is all part of the remembrance process. You are putting together this complex puzzle piece by piece as more and more of the collective begin to understand and work together rather than separately.

This can also feel uncomfortable and challenging to those who are fighting hard to keep things as they are. Because being closer to Source energy, and raising the frequency of the collective, brings you back to your oneness, and this means less control for the individual and more of a collective togetherness energy based on what is best for the all rather than the individual.

So, just as an individual who is not on their correct soul path witnesses more and more challenges in their life, the same goes for the collective. Imagine the collective as a single entity. One consciousness. This entity is wanting to go in one specific direction, but it is being pulled into the opposite direction instead. Using the river analogy again, this entity called 'the collective' begins to swim upstream rather than letting go and allowing things to go where it is meant to go naturally.

While swimming upstream, you are swimming against the current, and therefore it is a massive struggle as you fight against it. Just as you would experience as an individual being guided to your correct path, the same is for the collective as a whole. Fighting against the current creates challenging situations and with the big challenge comes the emotions of fear of losing control, desperation to hold onto what was, and fighting to keep things from moving forward.

This is what you are currently feeling as a collective. Puzzle pieces are being put into place by those who are ready to understand, but the process is slowed down by those fighting the inevitable and refuse to join the others.

Do not fear this shift, it is a beautiful thing. It may feel uncomfortable and challenging to deal with those who are fighting this frequency shift, but they will understand eventually just as you have. All of your lifetimes you have lived have been leading up to this exact moment. Each lifetime, though happening all at once, has propelled you into this level of mastery.

Keep placing those puzzle pieces down. Do not give up on raising the frequency of the collective no matter how hopeless it can feel at times. Remember, no one can swim upstream for long before they get tired and decide to let go, flowing with the current rather than against. Those who are fighting this shift are desperately wanting to hold onto their power, but again, power is in the collective as a whole, not the individual as some choose to believe.

Spread your light and love to everyone you meet, even those who may think differently than you. Everyone that is on this planet already has the seed planted from other lifetimes. Your light and love is the water for that seed to grow. Everything is happening for a purpose and for the collective's highest good. It may not feel like that always, but in order for beautiful plants to grow, there must be rain.

Your own love and light are your own umbrella and shelter from the storm. The storm will pass. It is inevitable that your puzzle you have all started together will be

completed. You are doing incredible work, friends, and you are witnessing the beginning of a new dawn. Trust and believe.

As always, we love you very much, brave ones, and thank you so much for listening."

WHISPER XLVIII:

The Illusion of Hierarchy

December 20th, 2025

"Hello, dear friends. We are back today to talk to you about hierarchy. Where does hierarchy come from? Let us discuss this. Human beings must place themselves on pedestals above others. This is what creates hierarchy. Someone who is in charge, someone who puts themselves in charge. Then, because they are at the top of this pyramid, let us call it, there must be others beneath them; and then there must be people beneath them and so on and so on, depending on how powerful the people are.

It could be about materialism or money. It could be what family you happen to have been born into. It could be several things. However, human beings place themselves in this pyramid of power. The most powerful person or persons at the top; a very, very small percentage. Then it moves downward to the people who are less influential, less powerful, and so on. This continues until you get to what the collective would consider the bottom. And what is the bottom? Human beings place those with no power and no influence at the bottom.

You have created this hierarchy system. To prove to each other who is more powerful, who is more influential, who has more control. That is what human beings do, have done, since the beginning. And those who are on a lower section of the pyramid, look to those that they feel are above them. Because they feel they have no control or power over their own lives, and they have placed their own control and power into somebody else. They have become powerless individuals you see.

If you place others above yourself, they have power and control over you. When the reality of it all is that all of you are equal. There is no hierarchy. You understand? It was simply made up. Created. You are all on the same playing field. No one is better than another. You are simply all learning different lessons in this particular lifetime. You are learning in all lifetimes, but we are speaking of this one that you are currently living in this moment as you are reading this.

You are equals. The person next to you sitting on a bus, the person who may not be as fortunate as you monetarily or materialistically. They are your equals, because at a soul level, your higher self requires no materialism, requires no money. Therefore, you are all the same. Because you are all one, having this experience together.

Now, when you think of the spirit realm, the realms of the angels. When you think of Source itself, or you call it God; it does not matter what you call it. Source can be called many names. It is whatever you want it to be. Source is the creator of all that is, all that ever was, all that will be. Source is the creator of all universes and realms and dimensions, the creator of all that is. So, as human beings place hierarchies on themselves, you also place hierarchies within the spirit realm.

This typically begins with Source at the top of this pyramid that you have created, correct? Then, beneath Source come Archangels. Then under them, you have angels, and under them, you have spirit guides and so on. And where do you all put yourselves on this pyramid? You have placed yourselves at the bottom of the pyramid. You feel you are *just* souls. You have placed yourselves on the lowest part of this pyramid; deeming yourselves to be powerless, uninfluential, unimportant. But that is not true. It is, in fact, the opposite.

We are all on the same playing field. We are all equals; we are all one. There is no hierarchy. Source is not above us. Source is *among* us. Just as source is a creator. We are also creators because we are fractals of source itself, you see? You are a piece of Source and Source energy. How can Source be better than itself? It cannot.

Everyone is equal. All things are equal. All dimensions, all spaces, everything is equal. Those you call angels, messengers, spirit guides, are equal. We simply all have different missions, different jobs as you would call them.

Is a doctor that performs surgeries more important than the mechanic that helps people with their vehicles? No. Both are equally necessary. You drive your cars every single day or ride your buses or transportation every single day. To keep them running, you must have these beings who are able to make sure your transportation is safe. That is a very important thing, yes? Same as a brain surgeon, who saves lives in that way. Both equal. Same as an entertainer who goes out on stage and performs and entertains is equally as important. Because without entertainment, without humor, survival would be nearly impossible.

Therefore, hierarchy is an illusion, created from the human mind. We are simply living in separate frequencies. And that does not make one better or one worse. It does not make one more powerful and one not so. Everyone has equal power, because we are all Source.

So, no more hierarchies. No more this person is better than me because of such and such. You are all equals. And as equals, it is our job to work together. To love each other. To support each other. To help each other. And how can you begin to help those around you today?

And, we leave you with that question. We love you so much, dear friends. We wish nothing but the best for you, you brave souls. And we thank you so much for listening."

WHISPER XLIX:

Protectors of the Plan

December 22ⁿᵈ, 2025

"Hello, dear friends. We are here today to talk about your protection. We have known you over lifetimes. We understand the contracts you have put together before your arrival on this planet. When you create your contract, it is very important that you stick to your original plan. This is so you do not get too far off track.

It is like going to school. When you take an English course, you expect that you will be taught English, not math or science. The same goes for your contracted life plan. There are certain lessons that you have put in place for yourself so that you can continue your soul's ascension plan.

This means that we cannot interfere with any life happenings that are a part of this plan. An uncalled-for intervention is like your parents removing you from class when you are in the middle of one of the most important class lessons, and then there is no way of relearning that lesson at that time. We cannot interfere with the lessons you have put in place for yourself.

However, we are constantly intervening within your life. Why do we do that? Since you must learn very specific lessons, and there are many of you inhabiting this simulation at once, we must make sure that nothing interferes with your plan. We are keepers of the contracts once the contracts are made. It is our responsibility to keep you on track, like a stage manager to a theatrical production. All must go as planned.

This means that if you are not meant to get a certain job because it would change the course of your life, we cannot allow you to get that job. If you are struggling to get to work, getting every single stop light, drive behind the slowest vehicles, and your frustrations are ever building - perhaps consider that we are preventing an event from occurring so that your life plan is not compromised.

Instead of looking at every negative situation that occurs to you on a daily basis as if it were a personal vendetta against you, we challenge you to look at things in another way. Consider that everything is working *for* you not *against*. Every major event that occurs in your life has been planned by you, and those must stay in place. However, we are always working behind the scenes to make sure your experience is moving in the correct direction.

We are protectors of your plan. Consider that if you did not go in the correct direction in your plan, and large life markers you had put in place did not happen, what would that mean? It would mean that you did not learn all the important lessons necessary to move forward, and you

would need to take the class again. We understand that human beings feel this simulation is their one and only reality, but it is only a small piece. If you were to have lifetime after lifetime with no cares in the world and everything is going right for you, what would you learn?

After many lifetimes of 'easy living' your higher self understands that it must have a mixture of both positive and negative events in order to really understand. Your soul is a sponge. It gathers and gathers data until it understands everything it can, and then returns to Source which is the ultimate ascension. Even we, who are speaking to you now, are still ascending as we continue to teach others and help others during their own ascension process. We are all equals.

Everything is working out for your highest good, even when it feels like the opposite. You could not come to this three-dimensional world without fully being prepared and ready to do it. It is very admirable and courageous.

There are many souls who are not ready for this experience you are having. They think they are ready, but they are not. It takes lifetimes upon lifetimes before one can truly be prepared for it. You are one of the select few. You are one of the select few because you are on Earth currently at this moment.

Instead of being frustrated or angry or fearful, try to figure out your own puzzle. Why were you meant to go through that specific event? What were you meant to learn? How did going through what you have in your human past benefit you later in life? Did it help you to appreciate relationships more? Did you grow from it?

Treat yourself like the student of life that you are, and begin to understand everything that has been laid out for you. Because, in reality, you created it for yourself for this process to not only learn from others and yourself but for you to teach others and yourself as well. We are all students and teachers at the same time.

We love you and your bravery very much, and we thank you so much for listening."

WHISPER L:

Free Will

December 24th, 2025

"Hello, dear friends. We are here today talk to you about the subject of free will. After our last message, it may seem that every major event in your lifetime is put in place by you before this incarnation, and that is true.

However, there is always room for improvising. Let us explain because it can seem complex, because it is. There is a lot happening not only within you and around you in your simulation, but also many things happening behind the scenes at the exact same time.

When you are here, and the Law of Forgetfulness is in place, you do not have a guide or map in front of you telling you where or how to go. This is where free will comes into play. To get from point A to point B, which we will consider large lifetime events, there are many ways to get to the destination.

If you look at a map and see all the roads that are present on the map, you will see that many roads can lead to the same place.

This is your free will. You have the free will to make many different choices on your travels. Some may be a more difficult path than the others. That is your choice. But that does not mean that we are not guiding you. We absolutely are at every point depending on the decisions you make.

You are guided by your intuition within you. This is that feeling and urge to do something that excites you. It slowly leads you to your purpose, many times bouncing from one bliss to another, which ultimately is still guiding you to your purpose.

If you draw two dots A and B on a piece of paper and separate them a bit, then draw a very squiggly, seismogram-like scribble, from dot A and eventually reaching dot B, that is much of how it works.

Regardless of how you get to a destination: by ways of the easier route or the more complex and complicated route, you will still get to that dot B that you put in place.

Guidance from us comes from not only that internal feeling that is pulling you, but also the outside of your control circumstances that occur. Things you cannot control: other humans around you, the weather, etc. There are different ways to keep you on track without you knowing anything about it.

We love analogies, so here is one: If you are driving your car and you have two roads you can go down. One road leads you a step closer to your purpose, the other leads in a direction you have taken before in other lifetimes, and you have already learned those lessons before, we will put up a road block. That road is now under construction, and you now have that one road to go down instead.

Even though you have the free will to choose how to get to a destination, if something will take you way off course where there is no hope of returning or finding your way back, we must block the road. This is not to hurt you but to help you.

Your soul is only interested in progressing not regressing, and if a certain road will not help you to progress and, in fact, does the opposite, we must protect your original intention.

However, if we see multiple roads ahead of you to choose from, and most of them will still keep you headed in the right direction, we do not mind which way you choose, but we will close off the roads that lead elsewhere. This does not mean that the road you choose will be easy. Some may be rough terrain, some may be slightly less challenging, it is really up to you. But you will get to your destination.

Some may say, "Then I will choose a road that is less likely so I can trick the system." That is only another road that will lead you to the same place. These major events you have planned for yourself must occur so that you can progress. Instead of worrying about tricking systems, follow your bliss. Your excitement. That is your guiding light. Follow what pulls you as long as it does not involve harming

anyone or yourself. That is a very important piece to understand.

That fire within you. Your internal pilot light. This is what should be driving you. Feel your way through life. If you have excitement about something you feel you must do, go down that road and discover what that is.

You can absolutely go in the opposite direction to 'trick the system,' but you will discover that you are unhappy, and you will eventually get back on track. It is really up to you. The script of life is written in bullet points, not word for word.

Each bullet point is a major event and lesson you are meant to learn or teach or both. So, we suggest following what gets you excited inside. Something that lights that fire within you, that pulls you forward. It is your guiding light.

If you are feeling lost, you may have taken a detour, but you are not off track. You are still heading in the right direction. But look within you. What do you want? What excites you? Start to feel your way through it and you will see a better road more clearly. We hope this helps you understand free will a bit more.

This was more of a continuation from the last message. There were questions about free will, and we wanted to address them promptly. We love you all very much, and we hope that this helped you. As always, thank you for listening. Farewell, friends."

A LETTER FROM YOUR REMEMBERED SELF

Dearest One,

I speak to you now from remembering, not distance. I am you without the forgetting. You once questioned whether the inner signal was real. It was. You were never imagining the connection – you were sensing your true nature.

You were never alone. The connection never broke; only your awareness of it dimmed at times. What you called seeking was returning. What you called growth was uncovering the light already within you.

You did not need to become worthy – you are the lantern. Awakening is not gaining something new, but recognizing what has always been true. You do not carry the flame. You are the flame.

There is nothing to prove and nothing to chase. Trust your inner knowing more than outer noise. You are not behind.

I am not ahead of you in time – I am you, remembered. The Infinite you reached for lives within you now.

Burn gently. Remain steady. Shine naturally.

— You

CONTINUE YOUR JOURNEY

Thank you for walking with me through these channeled messages I received. Remember, your soul's path is ever-unfolding, and you are never alone on the journey.

If you feel called to go deeper, I invite you to visit my website and YouTube channel:

www.GetKevInsight.com

www.youtube.com/@GetKevInsight

There you'll find information about me, my readings and guidance, my books, and any updates.

On my YouTube channel, you'll hear vocal channelings I've received among other videos I make.

May this be the beginning of an even greater unfolding in your life.

With love, light, and gratitude,

Kevin Wiczer